T0208335

THE HUMAN CONDITION

A PATHWAY TO
PEACE AND FULFILLMENT

BOB YARI

authorHOUSE®

AuthorHouse™
1663 Liberty Drive
Bloomington, IN 47403
www.authorhouse.com
Phone: 833-262-8899

Published by AuthorHouse 05/27/2021

ISBN: 978-1-6655-2229-8 (sc)
ISBN: 978-1-6655-2230-4 (hc)
ISBN: 978-1-6655-2228-1 (e)

Library of Congress Control Number: 2021907250

For Touran, Parviz, and Nina

CONTENTS

FOREWORD

As a species of life, we are conceived with certain propensities, needs and desires, and certain instinctive reactivity mixed into our emotional makeup. We can look at this as our natural genetic "programming." If analyzed objectively, we can see that this programming or our natural condition is a logical extension of the design of our species. It is there to enhance the species' survivability and aid its ability to progress. We have "urges" that give rise to our actions. Some of these are life sustaining; others have important purposes to drive us forward to advance learning and to better our species. Our urge to eat and our desire to mate is so powerful, it literally will overtake our rational thought processes and demand action on its own.

But some of our natural programming or instinctive behavior that served a valuable purpose at some point in our evolution can now impede the quality of our lives. Our propensity to over-eat, our instinctive fears of the unknown, and our urge to strike out with physical violence when angered, among many others are some of the tendencies that may have served our more primitive ancestors but may now needlessly do us harm in our modern existence. The advancements in our knowledge base and life circumstances makes some of our instinctive behaviors obsolete and unrewarding. This same progress in our learning also gives us the ability to re-program our own minds with the power of our thought and logic to better our lives and to experience a richer journey through our time-limited gift of life. The following chapters explore some of the ways we can modify our own propensities, moving beyond our natural programming or instincts to better enjoy our lives.

The below views considers our own human design, our "human condition" so to speak, and then explores some thoughts on living a better and happier life. There is so much we can take control of in our lives by adjusting our views, attitudes and our responses to external stimuli. We absolutely have the ability to enhance our own existential experience through the use of our powerful minds to adjust. All of us can modify our natural instinctive reactions and behaviors. This book is dedicated to exploring a philosophical shift in our thinking.

If there is an overriding message in this writing, it is that the most important feature we must nurture in ourselves is openness and open-mindedness. However much we may believe in our own views and ideologies, we must respect the right of others to believe differently. Both for their sake and ours, we must remain receptive and open-minded in our consideration of others' views.

With active thought and open-minded consideration, we can learn to break the constraints and bias of our influenced beliefs. We can free our thinking from the preconceived beliefs we have accepted from early on in our lives without much deliberate and rational filtration. Beliefs that often have no foundation in logic and fact. Only then can we truly explore our world and the wonders that abound around us and form educated and rational decisions that we have arrived at purely by and for *ourselves*. This, in and of itself, is one of the great gifts of life.

Respecting others' right to have views different from ours and being tolerant of those views is a hallmark of civilization. It is part of the human condition to be compelled to grasp onto an existing ideology and to absorb its beliefs into our own sense of identity. It's a condition that, combined with the fact that we are easily influenced in our formative learning years, makes changing handed down belief systems a difficult proposition. In this way, religious beliefs, ideologies, and certain prejudices have continued through generations on a steadfast, unalterable course. Despite this propensity, mankind's power of thought and logic gives us the ability to step back from our "influenced" learning and some of our innate primal instincts. And to then peruse our world, and the multitude of concepts in it, through rational and objective assessment. With deliberate effort, we have the ability to evaluate any concept without preconceptions or prejudices and to find the path to truth through the rule of logic.

In summary, it is my hope that this writing will inspire others to open their horizons and release the inherent, and often unused, powers of their own minds to better their lives and to continue our great quest of human learning. We live in an incredibly exciting time in the evolution of mankind. Our learning and knowledge base are increasing exponentially. We are at the dawn of our great advancement as a species. We are slowly getting closer to learning the universal "truths."

CHAPTER 1

I Don't Know

"I don't know." It's a simple phrase our human mind doesn't like much. It's toxic to human self-importance and self-value. We tend to never use it. Rather, we "know" by accepting or adopting a view, usually someone else's point of view. We listen to the various possibilities and other people's points of view and make a choice of what to make "our own" belief. And we often adopt an entire body of beliefs "wholesale," without any rational filtration. Naturally, we are influenced by our mentors, our social environment and, most dramatically, by the circumstances and atmosphere of our developmental years.

How many people do you know who believe in a religion different from the one they were raised in? Then, how many people do you know who are hardcore believers in the *same* religion that they were raised with? In short, almost all people, extremist believers, devout, or moderate, believe in the religions cast upon them at birth. We believe in these types of environmentally absorbed views with a degree of confidence and certainty that is usually unwarranted. We most often fail to take the question at hand, a proposed ideology, and truly analyze it through careful thought, consideration, and *factual* analysis. In other words, we fail to weigh what we truly know as fact and what we simply don't have enough information on which to render a decision. So, we tend to take a definitive position on issues even though we really shouldn't. At least, we shouldn't with excessive confidence and inflexibility. This leads to a common inability to simply say: "I don't know."

We have also come to rely on what we refer to as "gut feeling" on what is right and wrong, true or false. This is separate and distinct from our instinctive programming. It is based on what we've come to believe in multiple areas of our lives through our life experience. Gut feelings serve a real purpose. When we don't have facts or enough information to make a reason-based decision, the gut forms an opinion based on everything we've seen and learned to that point in our lives. However, we need to beware of the urge to answer all our questions with our "gut." Our cumulative learning and belief systems are often derived without factual analysis. They are usually based on other people's views that have been dictated to us. These are the beliefs that provides much of the foundation of our "gut" decisions.

Not to say that the gut feeling is always wrong. Sometimes that "intuition" is the result of learning that is based in truth and actual experience and therefore it can provide us with beneficial decision-making in certain cases, especially when quick decision-making is required. But since it is also based on beliefs that are unfiltered and adopted at a young age, it is usually highly biased and often incorrect. When we have ample time to evaluate, every question and every issue we ponder should be factually analyzed with complete benefit of the doubt being given to opposing views. Only fact-based assessment should drive us to an answer we are sure of. If none of that is available or if time is a factor, then resorting to the "gut" may help us.

We tend to believe in views, adopted at various stages of life, largely influenced on this great bias affected by our upbringing. If after we assess an issue factually and scientifically, we don't have an answer, we should be comfortable saying "I don't know." This doesn't mean we are not entitled to make choices and to develop beliefs without having everything factually verified. It's certainly normal and acceptable for us to develop unproven views when rational thinking and even some good evidence support conclusions to some level. That has been the basis of many great scientific discoveries. We propose a hypothesis and then we endeavor to prove or disprove it based on logical and factual analysis. But if there is a lack of fact and knowledge, we should be able to make our assessment and then simply say, "I don't know."

At the very least, we should be able to adopt a position or hypothesis and be very willing and open to modify our thinking in the face of more concrete rationalization or new evidence. Maybe we should simply avoid being so vehemently sure of our position even if our gut tends to favor one conclusion over another. By way of example, when the question of God comes up, how often do you hear someone say, "I don't know"? Almost never. But we really *don't* know. Yet we will say we are firm believers in God, almost always the God set forth by the religions into which we were born. Or we will say that we are atheists and that there is no God. Whether we have taken these conclusions from religious teachings or drawn them from scientific schools of thought (those who theorize life was developed through evolution) some of us are fastidious in our beliefs and will defend them vehemently even though, in truth, we cannot "know" the answer. If we are honest with ourselves, we should be able to say, "I don't know." We can acknowledge that overall truth even if we tend to believe a particular theory or school of thought for varying reasons.

CHAPTER 2

CONSCIOUSNESS

I think, therefore I am. As the dominant intelligent being on our planet, we certainly know *we* have consciousness. We process information, we think, we plan, we learn, we ponder, we feel. We exist in our minds and we can interact with and manipulate our world. What about other creatures? Does a dog have consciousness? A whale? An ant? Intuitively, I think everyone believes a dog has consciousness. We can see it in their eyes. They feel, they long, they anticipate, and even plan in very rudimentary ways. Do they have active thoughts? Their intelligence level certainly doesn't allow them to understand higher mathematics. But they can do many of the things our intelligence allows us to do.

Does consciousness require a certain level of intelligence (or vice versa)? I think if a being can perceive its surroundings with awareness, react with its environment, and manipulate that environment with decision-making, it must have *some* level of consciousness. I think the key word is "level." We have a higher level of consciousness than a dog and a dog has a higher level of consciousness than an ant. The ant largely responds to its environment with preprogrammed behavior. It makes very limited choices in its life, but it must have a basic sense of itself as it wanders through its environment, robotically doing what it is compelled to do. Do they have internal thoughts? Do they have emotions? Do they have an understanding that they are alive? Can consciousness be correlated to intelligence?

So, if we believe there are varying levels of consciousness below us, are there levels beyond and above us? If we believe in a Creator, intelligent enough to design this life on earth in its various forms, this life that is able to evolve, learn and continue indefinitely, what level of consciousness does this massively intelligent being hold? How is its awareness different from ours? We can only imagine what that level of awareness in our universe must be like.

What is consciousness? How do we become who we are, observing the world from our unique perspective and interacting with our environments? How is it that we are the one inside our minds looking outward? As the brain initially develops, it is also creating a completely unique set of criteria that becomes the unique individual in a world of billions. These varying criteria must include certain naturally engrained (preprogrammed) personality traits, an intelligence level and some propensity toward a specific emotional make-up. Then there are the effects our brains collect from our environmental realities as we grow. And maybe there is something external that powers the individual consciousness, like a soul. Or maybe not.

Each of our brains is unique in its composition of all its remarkable components. That must be what creates our individual consciousness. It can't be the other genetic traits that make us up, like physical traits. Our noses, our color, and possibly even our sex may not be material to who resides in our heads, so to speak. We can still be this same person and have a multitude of physical character traits. So, if not for a "soul," it truly must be that creation has provided for the brain to randomly configure between a variability that must number in the many trillions, to create a unique individual with a unique consciousness and identity. We are certainly then further shaped and formed as people by our life experiences and environments. But we must start with this very unique iteration of a physical human brain that is uniquely the individual that is us.

The questions of our universe are wide and profound. We are only now beginning to scratch the surface of going beyond our own perceptional limitations as human beings. We as an intelligent race have a very narrow set of tools to perceive and to interact with our universe. We "see" only with the limited visible light spectrum, we hear only waves created through air, we smell limited molecular emittances, we taste even more limited textures, and we finally can sense through touch. This touch allows us to conform the "real" nature of the state of matter around us to the picture the brain creates in our minds of what we *think* is our surroundings. In actuality, our brain creates a partial reality for us by creating a picture from the limited available data it has access to. This data comes primarily from electrical signals sent from the eyes to the brain. The eyes don't send a "picture." The brain receives electrical signals and, through a miraculous internal process, interprets them into a mental three-dimensional picture. This picture we have is only one version, or interpretation, of the reality around us.

Why are our dreams so real sometimes? Why do certain mental illnesses like psychosis create such realistic delusional worlds for some? Because the brain is using its same ability to create a picture world that it uses while we're fully awake and perceiving our "real" world. This is the world us humans experience, live in, and share. We know no other reality. However, with the advent of infrared imagery, spectral photography, and other systems, we have been able to get a small insight into how our environment may look to a being with different perception organs. Our environment and world would look vastly different as we changed our perception organs. Imagine a being that could only "see" heat variations and not detect the visible light spectrum. The picture created in their brain would show a vastly different world.

So, this "picture" we live in and share with most of our fellow animals is a mental picture based solely on the available perceptive senses we possess. We now know there are many other realities all around us that we cannot perceive biologically. Some of these we became very aware of early on. We cannot see the air, but we can feel its presence and see its effects. We cannot see electricity, but we can see lightning. Other realities which exist in our environment, we just have no senses to perceive at all and must rely on sensors we design and create to "perceive" them for us. Two of these, one nuclear radiation and the other radio waves or electromagnetic radiation, are now known to us. Although we have no bodily perception tools capable of experiencing these, we now know both flow all around us in great density, primarily from the sun. And, as we have partially mastered their utility, our own modern usage has increased the abundance of these elements all around us without any ability to sense their presence without manufactured instruments.

We now can communicate with instruments we have landed on Mars many millions of miles away using something we didn't know existed all around and all over us for many millennia. How many other unknown and unperceivable (to us) "things" exist around us? Our realities are structured by only the things we can perceive. I believe in time we will find more and more of, as of yet, undefined realities that are all around us and in some manner affect our existence and that of the greater universe. These may be things we cannot even conceive of with our current knowledge base. So, again, our picture of our surroundings would look very, very different with various added and subtracted "perception" abilities.

What is really happening, what the "true" real picture is, we can't currently know. We can only see our partial "representation" as the picture in our minds, and we can only imagine what we now know *is* there but that we cannot directly perceive. It's important to acknowledge our natural inabilities. It enables us to think differently. It allows us to move beyond the idea that reality is equal to our reality, that which we can perceive. Once we start believing that, it will greatly widen our horizons of learning.

In the continual process of technology freeing us from our biological limits, we are now able to gaze deep into the cosmos and the universe. We have seen new and fascinating things through our limited resource of visible light. With our added ability to detect radiation and electromagnetic energy (using newly devised instruments), we have added an additional layer to what we can perceive from this cosmic gazing. But again, what is out there that we have no bodily senses nor invented instrumentation to perceive? What elements we cannot even conceive of fill the universe? Bending time and space in a manner we don't yet understand. Possibly unknown elements that provide a foundation for other lifeforms or intelligences. We truly know very little of what the universe holds as we simply have massive restrictions in our ability to perceive, as proven to us by the relatively new realizations discussed above. We are just scratching the surface. The mysteries of the universe are still way beyond our comprehension. We currently theorize about much of the effects we see with our available instruments. But in reality, we just don't know what's there before our "eyes" but that remains unseen.

I don't know who it's originally to be attributed to but this saying goes back to the time of Socrates. Essentially, that there are the three "knowns". We know what we know. We know what we don't know. But we cannot know what we don't know we don't know. If something does not lead to an inconsistency or visible void, we will likely not suspect the gaps in our understanding and knowledge.

And how do our human emotions comprise a component of consciousness? Aside from our information processing abilities, our brains have been equipped with a large range of emotions. Who we are as individual human beings is highly influenced by our emotional composition. The emotional components of our minds are triggered and activated through chemical releases and absorptions in specialized areas of the brain. Some are need based, like our feeling of hunger, our feeling of lust, or our feeling of love. These are key to assuring the continuation of the species as they relate directly to maintaining life and reproducing life. Other emotions are environmentally stimulated. They are triggered by external realities. Anger, hatred, ambition, and curiosity represent just a few. These all serve their own purposes in compelling mankind to both advance itself and continue the species. Emotions are also part of our programming. Part of our human condition. In fact, some of our human feelings and emotions are purely human and appear in no other lifeforms on earth. Our emotions are intertwined with the processes of our thinking mind in a chemical symphony within our brains. Although we can now identify areas of the brain that respond to emotional stimuli through brain scans, we really know very little about how our brains process and create emotions. Are emotions part of a higher consciousness? They certainly are a critical part of our self-awareness and thought processes. We are in essence emotional beings and our various levels of emotional reactivity are an integral part of who we are as individuals.

Among our significant recent advancements in the last century, we have created "computers". Machines that can intake data and process that data with internal programming we have designed or "written" for them. Much like our own brain can take data and "process" it. These computers currently can't come close to our ability to mull and ponder, invent and create. But they do have a cursory ability to compare and sort information. As these computers are given more ability to process through more clever programs we create and are given access to even more sources to acquire data, will they develop consciousness? Will they start to think? What if we are able to program emotions into their function? It's certainly possible unless we believe there is another factor responsible for our own consciousness. Like a "soul" perhaps. We *are* going to find out, someday.

As we design more and more sophisticated processing machines, we will eventually find out if we are able to make them think, create, feel emotions, and ponder on their own. Maybe then we will determine whether a soul is involved in our own consciousness if these machines can find consciousness through programming and processing alone. When we do create these machines, if they have these facets leading to consciousness, then reproducing them will possibly create a new race of being. It will still be unable to repair itself, reproduce itself, or physically manipulate its world. But how far behind could that be? We are nowhere near being able to recreate this system of emotions in our computers with electrical currents and binary codes. But will we be able to do so once we have cracked the secrets of the emotional response system and have found out how to emulate nature's four-element data storage and coding system?

I believe we will get there. We are acquiring knowledge at an accelerating pace and the functioning system in its entirety is clearly there for us to decipher. And then we'll be one step closer to being able to create consciousness within our own creations. Remember, all the information is here in front of us in our own tiny cells, the trillions of bits of data that can show us how to build a continuing lifeform *with* consciousness. We just don't have the advancements in our science and knowledge needed to decode and understand it at this point in our evolution.

In the future, advancements in our knowledge of cell reproduction and its programming will allow us to make certain materials (from human skin to food packaging) from organic elements grown for specific purposes. As we slowly unfold the secrets of our cells, we will be able to build more and more sophisticated machines of our own with unimaginable capabilities. If we survive long enough as a species, we may even be able to design our own new lifeforms. Hopefully, by such time our degree of maturity and scientific responsibility will have grown equally sophisticated so we don't jeopardize the intricate natural balances and threaten the entire ecosystem, including our own existence. We currently live in a period of time where our technology and science is ahead of our collective maturity in being able to responsibly manage our world, such that we live with a constant threat of annihilating ourselves.

CHAPTER 3

THE HUMAN MIND - MACHINE WITH CONSCIOUSNESS

The human mind is a miracle. It is an island in a sea of perceived reality. The brain is thrust into consciousness with pre-programmed instinctive behavior, the ability to store memory, the ability to receive information from its surrounding, and the capacity to transform this information into possibilities. It then has the ability to evaluate options, choose and act on decisions, manipulating and building from its environment. The basic powers of the mind allow it to grow, to learn, to quest for knowledge, power, and progress. Our instinctive behavior or biological programming is manifest in our strong needs and desires.

We are compelled to do certain things that are key to the survival of our species without the need for much rationale thought. We don't need rationale thought to reproduce or to take in sustenance; we are compelled to take the actions required by our programming. In fact, our rational control is hardly able to stop these processes. Our natural programming often overrides our decision-making mental processes. Some of this natural programming is less over-powering but just as determinative of our actions. Our propensity to anger and to fight, our tendencies toward fear and flight, and our protectiveness over our own are just a few examples. This programming is essential to the continuity of life.

However, as we grow wiser and more advanced, some of these tendencies and behaviors are not as beneficial as they were for our less knowledgeable and less advanced predecessor generations. For various reasons, some of these instinctive response systems now tend to hurt or limit our species in our evolving world of progress. A simple example would be our tendency to over-eat even though, if our logic was in full control, we would stop when we are reasonably full. Our primal instinct is to eat as much as possible to store energy when food is available since in primitive times, we may not have always had access to a timely next meal. But in our modern world, we don't need to store excess calories as food is relatively abundant. Likewise, we are "compelled" to do many other things that may have been important at some point in our evolution but are now less than desirable attributes. We do have the ability to modify these potentially harmful tendencies in our instinctive programming. We will discuss some of these in later chapters.

Yet past a set of very primal abilities (including our natural programming), the mind is completely dependent on the internal "building" of more advanced processes by the conscious mind itself. Education (the passing of information garnered by prior generations through concentrated learning) has been the backbone of this process and has enabled man to accelerate his progress by leaps and bounds over the last millennium. Over thousands of years, human learning has been handed down generation to generation by one-on-one teaching or apprenticeships. Much of what a generation learned was lost, and what was passed down was passed down to a limited few. Those that received the information, usually didn't receive it due to merit or ability. With this methodology, human progress was slow. But then came books and the printing press. Suddenly, not only was information able to be recorded to go past a single generation, it was also mass-produced by the printing press. This then made generational learning and discoveries available to the masses of the next generations. The new generations became capable of garnering the knowledge of previous generations and building upon it based on each individual's area of interest. Learning and progress in our knowledge increased exponentially and gave us tremendous advancements over the last two centuries. This condensed educating of the human mind enables it to create and advance at far greater levels than the raw human mind would allow.

However, education can take place with two separate and distinct methods. The memorizing of information as a foundation for future learning and building is linear as opposed to logarithmic. As we memorize, we do learn and we are able to work in advancement of specific specialized areas of knowledge. But ultimately, this method is limited. True creativity and progress upon knowledge is made by true *comprehension* of knowledge. Understanding of prior conclusions is essential. When we truly understand concepts, we can add tremendously more with our own thought processes. It is this understanding that allows us to build our own internal mental processes to better function, absorb, and create new information. The bottom line is that, once education is available, it is up to us how we learn from these resources and also how we modify our mental functions to handle and process the information. Rote learning is useful, but it is a far less desirable method to deep comprehension of core concepts.

A simple example is a rudimentary physics equation defining force, F=MA. Force is defined by a mass being accelerated through space. It's a relatively simple equation but a complex concept to truly comprehend as it doesn't readily appear to be true in our earthly environment due to our atmosphere. As we are overpowered by earth's gravity in our biological existence, we can't apply a small force to an object and have it move continuously at constant speed. We need to go into space for that. We can "learn" this concept by memorizing the equation. We can then use it, plug variable numbers into it and extract useful results. We can make a career out of the science of physics and we can lead a useful life that in turn adds to human advancement in various ways. But if we *understand* what that equation means so we truly comprehend that definition of force and how it relates to accelerating (not continuing at constant speed) a mass, we can then apply the mind in a whole new manner and possibly add to the knowledge base of physics. It takes a different level of interest and fascination with a subject to really want to understand its concepts as opposed to simply memorizing them.

The same is true for the comprehension of our own human condition. As we learn more and more about our own programmed behaviors and their logical functions toward the survival and advancement of our race, the more we really comprehend and deeply understand these functions, the better equipped we are to modify and adjust these natural tendencies in our favor.

In learning to manipulate our minds to better function in the processes of learning and to modify our thinking to better our lives, we need to expend mental energies in internal analysis and step-by-step self-improvement. This is not an instinctively natural process. The natural process is to simply gain information, memorize it, add to it, choose what is "right" and utilize it. And ultimately pass it on to the next generation. However, to sit back and to analyze how our mind handles information and thought and how we can improve our own mental functioning is an act that requires advanced and forced steps. The first is to step outside ourselves and our immersion in our spectrum of life and to look upon life, ourselves, our functioning, and our purpose objectively.

If we truly step "outside" of our perceived communal world, we can look down upon ourselves and recognize that we are basically machines. Sophisticated, chemical-based, self-regenerating, self-powering computers. Computers with the addition of a set of complex emotional responses and measures. We begin as sponges for the data of the world around us and the teachings of our prior generations. We are then programmed to build upon what we learn and create new paths and horizons to advance on. The more we understand our own mental make-up, the better we will become at managing and controlling our own lives. Our minds contain three distinctive "departments." Whether we call them id, ego, conscious, subconscious or whatever, the basic departments generally fall into the same categories.

First is our "automated" department where no thought takes place. Here we are pre-wired to handle bodily functions and to respond with pre-programmed instincts. We have limited conscious access to this area. Let's call this the "automated mind." This department of the mind contains our pre-programming at birth. An example of this is our "instinctive" response of closing our eyelids as an object approaches our eye, even right after birth. The automated mind can only be programmed (outside of its original pre-birth programming) with a degree of constant repetition such that it "learns" the repeated function in its automated mode and stores this information in the memory. An example of this might be the way we tie our shoelaces, ride a bicycle, or hit a tennis ball, skilled activities without conscious thought after we initially "learn" them. In reality, it's the automated mind that's really learning these primarily motor skills, with no further active thought required for our bodies to perform the task.

The second department of the mind is the memory, which is basically a storage facility for all our memories. Here *all* data received by the senses and the conclusions reached by the mind internally are stored in a tiered fashion. More important memories are stored in readily accessible areas and the less important memories are stored deep in a less accessible area. We'll call this simply "the memory."

The third department of the mind is the "thinking" or conscious mind. Here (the prefrontal cortex center), information, both from direct input of our senses and from the memory, is "processed" in combination with our emotions. "Processed" is a function where data is lumped in a grouping of information and assigned a level of importance. It is then viewed in conjunction with other groupings of information and the mind makes decisions, balancing information against each other and making choices between them in convergence with our emotional responses. All information, once options are decided upon, are built into more and more complex sets of information and sent to the memory for future use against new information. This process leads to creativity and invention as we "ponder" new information against our stored memories relevant to the topic of the new information and we then weigh, balance and explore the relationships between these sets of information. This also creates our internal voice which we then ponder and explore with language in a voice only we "hear." Let's call this the "thinking mind."

Earlier, we briefly discussed our very human emotions. These chemical reactions within the brain are primarily connected to our thinking mind. Our emotions directly trigger and interact with our thought processes, influencing them greatly. They are intertwined with our processing of new information against our stored memories. The automated mind is relatively oblivious to our emotions. It does trigger emotions to a certain extent with reactions like "fight or flight," so there definitely are certain connections, as is true for all areas of the brain. But it is primarily our thinking mind that stores its memories of emotional events to the memory so we can recall and refine our emotional responses with deliberate thought. Our emotions are a critical part of our brains and a critical part of our being. Unlike the ant that largely acts pursuant to pure instinct (its natural programming), we are largely driven to act and behave pursuant to our emotional responses and triggers. We are emotional beings. We are computers with instinctive programming and emotions that guide us through our lives.

Communication between the departments differs immensely. Both the thinking mind and the automated mind have communication with the memory, but it is the thinking mind that has the most broad access to memory recall and input. The thinking mind finds relevant information when it is needed, either due to new information being learned or internal thought about a topic. Once these memories are retrieved, it is the thinking mind that will start the process of weighing, comparing, and assessing the collective information together. In contrast, the automated mind has instant access to the memory for its naturally programmed duties and for those that it has "learned" and has stored in the memory. It doesn't seem to have much use for the memories created by the conscious mind. With repeated actions, the automated mind creates its own memories unavailable to the conscious mind, such as how we actually ride and balance on a bicycle.

The most complicated communication is between the thinking mind and the automated mind. As stated above, the automated mind can readily access the memory and find the programmed actions that it learned from active repetitions from its experiences and also from programming built into the brain prior to birth (our natural instincts). These programmed memories of the automated mind are available to the thinking mind without any thought other than to trigger the programmed action. So, we get on a bicycle and we don't have to think about how to ride a bike and we don't need to take appropriate actions consciously. The automated mind takes over the task and instructs the body as needed, without our even realizing it. How often have you gotten into your car, and, while engaged in other thoughts, ended up driving somewhere you didn't intend to but had done so many times before? Your automated mind is doing most of the driving. The conscious mind will interject and make its will known, but if it wanders off, the automated mind takes over completely and drives us where it thinks we're going from repetition.

However, the thinking mind cannot "think" a program into the automated mind, nor can it alter its functions through its thoughts. In certain ways, the difficulty in communication between these two departments is exasperated by the internal "noise" between them. The "noise" being electrical activity in the brain that is the result of the senses sending externally derived information from our sensory organs to the brain along with our emotional reactions to these stimuli. And therefore, as we "quiet" these noises, by reducing external stimuli to the brain, we can facilitate a channel of communication between our thinking mind and our awesomely powerful automated mind.

Accordingly, we actually do have an ability to "program" our automated mind outside the normal way in which it learns. Our thinking mind can initiate a programming of the automated mind by using repetition while inducing a "state" in our minds where internal noise is reduced and communication is facilitated. This condition has been practiced for many years by those who practice hypnotism, self-hypnotism, meditation, visualization techniques, and many other disciplines. All of these concentrate the mind on relaxation and the reduction of communication with the surrounding world, thereby reducing the electric currents in the mind. Once this state is induced, the conscious mind can more readily communicate with and program the automated mind. Or someone externally can do so by acting as the voice of the thinking mind, which is basically hypnosis. Again, this programming is generally done with repetition. As we train in life for different activities, sports and skills, this is what is happening. We are largely training our subconscious mind to handle much of the tasks we want to master. The automated mind "learns" by repetition, so once we access a clear line of communication, we must set up a repetitive course of what we want programmed. Once the automated mind receives new "programming," it then adjusts its control over our physical bodies or our memory to conform. This means that we can program our automated mind to make us better athletes, to be more relaxed and in control of our lives, to quit smoking, give up bad habits, etc. The power of these techniques is only beginning to see the light of day. I believe in the coming years, we will utilize this science more and more to better ourselves and empower ourselves, enhancing the quality of life. In the future, these disciplines will be routine exercises of our daily lives, especially self-hypnosis, where we can access the power of the automated mind without external assistance.

Again, our mind is relatively similar to our own man-made computer. The mind collects data from external inputs, stores the data in both readily accessible memory and embedded memory, and it has a processor that manipulates this information and sends it to an output, the memory and/or the motor neurons. One of the greatest differences between our current computers and our minds is the ability of the mind to internally initiate processing from its stores of memorized information. The mind, in its prefrontal cortex, creates constant weighting of pieces of newly input and/or stored information against each other, mixed in with our emotional reactivity. The mind compares new information with stored information in the memory and then creates options that it will then decide upon. This decision-making revolving around these options will then be stored as memory. This constant learning and processing of the "learned" data along with our intricate range of emotions creates our thoughts and sense of consciousness.

Amongst other methodologies, we can therefore take actions to better ourselves through both main components of our minds. We can use self-hypnosis, or "self-programming," by using relaxation and repetition exercises to effect behaviors, skills, and attitudes to in effect modify our automated mind. And more powerfully, through our thinking mind, we can use deliberate thought and deeper comprehension to slowly adjust our reactions, attitudes, and outlooks to improve the quality of our lives.

We are at the infancy of both our understanding of the function of the mind and in our evolution with the computer. We will ultimately arrive at true "artificial intelligence" within the electrical medium. The computer will eventually "think" and learn on its own. It will then become a "being" in its own right. The human race has accelerated its progress in knowledge immensely in the past two hundred years. Again, this has been primarily due to its improved ability to store and communicate previously learned knowledge. Books and institutes of higher education have accelerated the next generation's learning ability by providing it with a wealth of densely compacted knowledge from which it could build new knowledge. So too will computers be able to both learn from their environments and harness the knowledge input to them by their human counterparts. Computers will be able to accelerate our own learning ability dramatically in this way.

CHAPTER 4

IMAGINATION

Imagination is a mechanism built into our human minds. As children, our imagination is activated by pretend play and role playing. We insert ourselves into roles we have perceived in our environments. We emulate being people we admire and who fascinated us. With imagination, we create scenarios and fabricate events. These "fabrications" are variations of what we have experienced and learned. In this way, we exercise our imaginative functions and hone our ability to manipulate our realities into various possibilities.

As we grow into adulthood, this skill lends itself into creativity and invention. We continue to use realities in our environments to mold and fabricate various possibilities. We imagine what *could* be possible. Accordingly, imagination is the source of our creativity and invention. It is a critically important part of our brain's ability to create progress.

Every invention started with someone's imagination transforming elements in our everyday lives into a novel use. We do this by using our knowledge and experience and applying it to "possibilities". Spears, the wheel, boats, and planes were all developed this way. But this imagination also invents myth and lore. To answer our unexplained questions of our world, we often use this imagination to conjure up causation and creators. Unfortunately, this process does not have the benefit of trial and error as a basis of verifying its truth. With inventions, we test an imagined possibility through physical fabrication and physical trial. If it works, it sticks. If it doesn't, it is discarded. When we don't have the ability to verify an imagined concept, we can simply believe something to be true with no basis in fact.

In this way, many religious and mystical beliefs have taken root and have been passed on through generations. They have become the answers to our questions about our planet, our lives and creation. If one person believes something, it is easily engrained into their offspring. Since in youth we are prone to accept, without question, what our parents and elders teach, beliefs can spread rapidly through the generations.

With our imagination we have molded our world. We have explored, created and built. We have traveled to other planets and sent our creations beyond our solar system. I believe the greatest thinkers of our time also had the most active and "wild" imaginations. Our "day dreaming" and fantasizing is therefore an incredibly important part of our ability to grow and evolve as a race. What starts out as pretend play ends up as an important tool to invent new concepts and creations.

As we exercise our ability to conjure up possibilities, we learn, we grow and we progress. Knowing the value of our imagination is a necessary acknowledgement to then allow ourselves to dream and imagine freely. Without our imagination, we may never have broken out beyond the lives lived by our cavemen ancestors.

CHAPTER 5

OUR NEED TO BELIEVE AND FOLLOW

We all start with an internal void compelling us to "believe" in something. In *what* hardly seems to matter. We desire "meaning" in life. Again, it is human programming, our human condition. We need to satiate a need to identify with a cause. We need to believe in something greater than ourselves so that we may promote and build upon that cause. It gives us a sense of purpose. It gives us a sense of being a part of something we can belong to. It makes us follow people we see as leaders, those "worthy of our support." We grab onto ideals and causes. These then become a part of us and they become part of our identity. We find comfort in believing and following. In part, this need makes us readily susceptible to believe in the religions that are fed to us at a young age.

In part, wrote Viktor Emil Frankl, this is because "Those who have a 'why' to live, can bear with almost any 'how.'" Frankl, a Holocaust survivor, neurologist, and psychiatrist who wrote the bestseller *Man's Search for Meaning*, asserted, "What man actually needs is not a tensionless state but rather the striving and struggling for some goal worthy of him. What he needs is not the discharge of tension at any cost, but the call of a potential meaning waiting to be fulfilled by him."

There is good reason for this bit of programming in us humans. It strengthens the bonds of the tribe and creates drive in us. We fight for our ideals and our tribe. And we become better and stronger as our tribes become stronger and grow to be able to defeat our rival tribes. All the while, presumably, we are "bettering" the human race in the process as the more fit and dominant endure.

This need to believe and belong is most pronounced during our coming of age to adulthood. In our late teenage years, we also are more prone to being rebellious, which is a manifestation of needing to subscribe to a cause of our own. When we are faced with this need and we have not found a connection with any compelling cause derived from our childhood, we are extremely vulnerable to jumping on the nearest bandwagon available especially if that particular bandwagon furthers our need for a separate identity from our status quo, which is typically identified with the circumstances and desires of our parents. This rebellious behavior is similar to mutations in evolution. It causes variance from the norm so that a new concept can be tested for its viability and superiority. If it "takes root," it will become the dominant superseder.

But this strong primal need is first manifest in our great propensity to accept deeply what we are spoon fed in our developmental years. Our beliefs and ideals are generally the same as those of our parents or other strong influencers during childhood. We tend to not question much of what we are taught in our early stages of life. And as we grow older, most of us tend to allow these unchallenged beliefs to gain even stronger roots within us, and we become more and more an advocate of what we were *told*. These ideals then become part of who we are and how we think. They become the foundation of our faith, our prejudices, and our values. It begins to define us. A consequence of this component of our human condition is that we lose our natural defense of being suspicious of what is being promoted to us. We fail to question. But we really should question just about everything for ourselves. We should give due consideration to other points of view and judge the logic of any concept or school of thought, no matter who is advocating for it. We should then make rational and logical judgments upon what we wish to believe. We should not simply accept things that are taught to us by someone else, however much we may respect them.

With this reality of our human condition, a majority of people came to believe in the God of religion. Primarily the God set forth by each person's childhood religion. We need faith for many reasons. Probably the most profound is our need to feel comfort and security in our own being with a greater guiding force watching over us. We also need to explain our very existence, where we are going, and what our responsibilities and parameters are. As science and knowledge provide more logical explanations of our surrounding world, our need for raw faith diminishes. However, where there was very limited knowledge, a great need existed to believe in a greater, benevolent being.

Is the brain hardwired for God? Neuroscientist Andrew B. Newberg, a prominent researcher in nuclear medical brain imaging and neurotheology, asserts that it does appear that the brain has "this profound ability to engage in religious and spiritual experiences, and that's part of why we've seen religion and spirituality be a part of human history."

Clinical psychologist Steven Reiss wrote, "What I'm trying to answer is the nature of why people embrace religion and God." His conclusion: "People are attracted to religion because it provides the opportunity to satisfy all their basic desires over and over again."

Throughout history, this human need manifested itself in many different forms of idols, gods and other heavenly inhabitants. Then Judaism introduced the concept of monotheism, one God, which spread as the generally accepted provider of all answers to our existential questions. Originally, most religions were a beneficial tool that was wisely used by leaders and intellectuals of the time to create the rules of social co-habitation. At a time when communal laws and social enforcement were non-existent, the laws of the jungle ruled the first human communities. Then came the notion of morality and guidelines for right and wrong, which were set forth as the will and ways of an almighty God.

It is interesting to objectively view the original religious laws set forth in this manner, such as the ten commandments. It is relatively apparent that these laws are primarily geared to allow communal living, in general peace, where people could raise a family, maintain their possessions (and therefore have motivation to work), and remain relatively free from aggression. Previous to these new standards promoted as the will of God himself, the rule of the strong prevailed. If you had greater strength, either in numbers or simply by being the strongest in the group, everything was yours for the taking: possessions, territory, the most desirable mates and ultimately leadership. But over time, wisdom and knowledge took over the rule of the strong by capitalizing on the great need to believe that exists in the human condition. The great unilateral acceptance of the concept of God made the very first rule of law possible in the human race.

This unusually useful concept slowly deteriorated into the battle of religions as more and more ambitious individuals and groups learned the power and influence they could exert by claiming to represent the will of this now widely accepted God. Religion quickly fell prey to new and wide-ranging agendas, such as accumulating power. New ideologies appeared, mostly stemming from the same

God, as the old cabals were firmly controlled by a hierarchy of men and gaining great strength. These new belief systems then formulated new rules, customs, and guidelines to differentiate themselves from the others and to hold their own members loyal to their "clubs." Interestingly enough, most of these newly formed religions held fast to the ideology of one God, which had now proven to be a successful concept. The great differences became who represented what, when, and by whom but they all led to the same God, just under a different name. Leaders encouraged blatant racism and hatred of other sects or religions. Killing, the very first prohibition of this God, instead took the form of acceptable behavior as long as it was part of a "holy" mission to destroy those who didn't believe in your religion. Man became blind to the forest for the trees. In one of the great ironies of human history, religion became a source of hatred and murder.

The concept of the one God became inseparably intertwined with these self-serving sects, all preaching the word of the same God and all claiming all forms of unsupported, scientifically improbable beliefs as to how God created *everything*, what he wanted, how he was to be worshiped, what he would reward, and what he would punish. Accordingly, with this haphazard and manipulative manner of defining God, the concept of "a Creator" generally contradicted the wisdom of scientific discovery, as it came. But, again, if we step out of our subjective constraints, and peel the layers of hyperbole off the mandates of religion, we will see that science can in fact support the existence of a Creator. Even if we reject the notion of the God promoted by religion, there is supportable evidence of a greater knowledge and force in the universe that may be responsible for the creation of life on earth. Religion continues to serve a great purpose in society notwithstanding its propensity for being abused to the detriment of humanity in many ways. The very core of almost all religion is kindness and forgiveness. It promotes family life, a sense of community, and cultural identity. Often these qualities are hidden by the modern layers of justification for hate, segregation, and violence laid by those abusing and manipulating the mass support of the religious machine. These more positive qualities serve the cause of peaceful co-habitation even when compared to our now matured rule of manmade law and order. Most religious people still promote and receive these great qualities from generation to generation, creating more civility in every corner of the world. One can only imagine the violence and conflict in a world without religion and its Godly commandments. As we look at our world today with its widespread war and violence, even with our current international laws, it could be much, much worse if morality had not been disseminated as it has by religion. And this is another good reason to still respect what others believe, despite what we may strongly believe ourselves.

With all the overall good religion does for society, unfortunately, it also has caused us to take leave of our logical exploration of our world and has confined us to the handed-down beliefs that religion tends to pound into our heads from an early age when we are most susceptible to being influenced. As we become a more educated and a more intelligent race, we should need the rote belief in religion less and less. We can therefore afford ourselves the freedom to explore, investigate, and find the truth of our world on our own. We can then become the untainted, pure canvass for finding the realities of our universe with the benefit of the scientific knowledge we have gathered throughout the centuries. We only need to look to our logic along with hard clues and evidence to formulate new theories and then set out to prove or disprove them. We can do all this and still belong to our respective religions for its beneficial qualities such as promoting community and family unity. We can still be a part of our religions and yet reject some of its views and teachings. We can respect our religions more as a culture rather than a wholesale belief system. If we do so, it would be so much easier to be accepting of other people's religions and views. Just as it seems we are generally more accepting of other people's nationalities, the differences start to diminish.

So, it's part of human nature to follow. Our human nature, our natural instinctive programming, dictates that some of us be leaders and that most of us be followers. We cannot all be leaders. We need leaders and we need them to be exceptional and strong. But we cannot have a world, of any particular species, where all its members are leaders. The logic is simple. To lead, you must have many followers. Some must lead, many must follow. Therefore, as the sheep follows its herd, our most basic instinct is to follow. We all suffer the sheep's syndrome. We are by nature compelled by forces beyond our intellectual control to believe in a cause and to grasp an ideology in its totality. In this magnificently simple way, each society will have its strong-minded individuals take the lead and put forth their will to their followers. They will offer their rope and others will grasp it and pull with all their might, putting the leader's agenda into motion.

Followers implement the will of the leaders. This component of human nature compels us to want to pick up and follow a belief or a cause. It also compels us to assign a symbol in the form of a person for our cause and to promote and follow this person in parallel with promotion of the cause. In many instances, the subject of our symbol becomes as important as the cause itself, often blurring the separations, so that we become truly subordinate and compliant to the wishes of another. These instinctive traits in a majority of humanity causes most of us to follow others. Very few of us are born leaders.

These people lack the following instinct and, instead, they possess the strong will and self-confidence to lead. However, most leaders are converted former followers. They take lessons from the leaders they experience as followers and transform themselves into leaders. We all have a bit of leader built deep into our natural programming. But it takes a certain amount of self-taught determination and drive to make the transition to leadership. Something we can all do with the right inspiration.

Such has been, and continues to be, the making of tribes, cults, clubs, brotherhoods, gangs, nations and religions. We are compelled to grasp an identity and bond with those who are the same as us in some fashion. A flock for protection and promotion. Once we are within the security of our "sameness" grouping, the outsiders become the enemy. Again, this logical mechanism tends to lead to the advancement of the stronger group and thus results in progress and better survivability for the species. Of all causes, nationalistic or otherwise, religion has best fed man's need to fulfill his follower instinct. What could be better than an all-powerful, unseen, and benevolent leader to follow? The very Creator of all mankind and everything else in existence. Dressed in the promise of heaven and other rewards for the faithful, man has eagerly swallowed the "teachings" of the greatest being of them all. It should be natural that such a being would not make himself known to us meager humans and that we should have representative messengers equipped with direct communication with the all-powerful to deliver his messages and instructions to us. We *need* to believe.

This is all part of the human condition and probably quite necessary for our survival and progress. However, it also leads us to believe too quickly and to accept the preaching of others too readily. We tend to suspend our own logic and reasoning in favor of adapting an existing philosophy wholesale. Even if we cannot all be leaders, we should think like leaders and be wary of leaders who promote ideas that are not acceptable to our logical minds after we apply logic and reason to analyze any proffered concepts.

My own personal feeling is that there is a Creator which is responsible for life on earth. This, as opposed to the theory that life was created by a chance event. I also believe it is highly probable that this Creator is vastly different from the God defined by our major religions. We truly don't know what a potential Creator may be or what form it may exist in. But a study of the facts surrounding life, the miracle of its core cellular machinery, and the intricate inter-dependent balances in nature, lead to a conclusion that's hard to refute. The conclusion that life was created by intelligent design. For an in-depth discussion and analysis of this concept, you can also read my book: "On Creation and the Origins of Life".

CHAPTER 6

THE NEED FOR ACCEPTANCE

As individual human beings, aside from the powerful need programmed into us to survive and continue the species (our instincts to eat and procreate, for example), our need for acceptance is possibly our greatest instinctive need. It is closely related to the instinctual need to be part of a tribe but a distinct need in and of itself. The need for acceptance guides every aspect and component of our lives. It makes us care about our appearance. It makes us want to succeed, to progress individually. It controls our behavior from the conformist behavior down to the revolutionary behavior. It is all to attract attention to "me." We want to be popular; we want to be known; we want to be special. We want to be desired by potential mates and admired by all others. Our self-esteem is commensurate to our perceived degree of acceptance.

Two components to one's general self-image or social self-esteem are physical self-image and status self-image. Each contributes to our overall self-esteem. Physical self-esteem is how we believe to be physically perceived by others. In other words, how "attractive" we are perceived to be. This is partly guided by society's norms and standards for physical attractiveness. We all, to some extent, work out, diet, dress well, and groom or apply makeup to enhance our physical desirability. Status self-esteem is how we believe we are perceived with respect to our "success" or status in life. In other words, how smart we are, how accomplished we are, what possessions we own, and what position we hold in society.

The combined self-esteem, directly effects our motivations in life and sets our goals and parameters. We always act in direct consideration to our self-esteem. We generally respond with two main types of behavior as a result of our self-esteem. One is a compensating action where we strive to fulfill the perceived short comings. We are motivated and strive to become better as we seek acceptance. Another, less positive reaction is to shrink from confronting opportunities perceived to be outside our reach due to perceived handicap. It is a debilitating force. We are not attractive enough so we dare not approach someone we are attracted to. We are not perceived as being smart by others so how can we get that job we dream about? We then don't try something challenging and rewarding because of what *we believe* others may think of us.

We tend to believe we are "important" when others believe we are "important" and we tend to believe similarly with every other component of our self-image. This is the basic essence of our need to be accepted. Again, this is a built-in mechanism. All people, more or less, are slaves to this natural phenomenon of the human condition. The acceptance and confirmation of others gives us security and self-worth. We strive to be admired and looked up to by others, known or unknown. This need drives us to match our worth against other people's "worth." As social animals, we look to those of our immediate environment, those most compatible with us, with which to judge ourselves against. This group is generally comprised of relatives, friends and work associates whom we deal with most regularly in our lives.

We start this process as children, competing in sports, comparing possessions and vying for physical dominance. The peers we designate in early life are often the circle of people we continue to evaluate our own successes and self-worth against. We generally do not compare ourselves to people either way above or way below our own perceived socio-economic status. We continue to use those we are familiar with in our own circles and those that we see as in our own relative range in the spectrum of life. We therefore tend to judge our worth from the perspective these people have of us. We always want to be ahead of *this* pack. Often, this also leads to the unfortunate human trait that causes us to want the failure of others in our "self-worth" group, as much as we want our own advancement and success. This is the result of quantitative comparison with our peer group's life positions rather than adopting a neutral frame of reference for our advancement. A standard which we can determine.

In many ways, this instinctive (preprogrammed) human behavior is a practical necessity as it drives us to strive for success and advancement regardless of where we stand in the socio-economic status spectrum. Even billionaires compete with each other and strive to gain more "worth." However, we would live more content lives were we to recognize this phenomenon and temper our judgment of ourselves against others with a more subjective view upon our "worth." The simple truth is that the opinion of others does not provide any basis for our "worth" even though it affects our own view of our self-worth. Spending less time worrying about what other people think and trying to improve their opinions of us will give us both inner peace and the ability to recognize that our true value is independent of other's opinions. Our "value" should be based on who we are as people, how kind we are, how loved we are by those close to us, and how we lead our lives. Our "worth" should be in how we judge ourselves against our own standards of decency and growth. Ultimately, it doesn't matter all that much what the "self-worth group" thinks; it matters what *we* think of ourselves and *that* is purely within our mental control, provided we learn to exercise such control.

Most importantly and most readily, we can reduce how much value we put on other people's opinions of us. Again, it takes conscious effort and self-training, but if we learn to live our lives without too much emphasis on what other people think, we will find a great freedom and reduction in stress. The less we care, the more we can actually do what makes us happy and not tie our happiness to what we actually only *perceive* to be what other people think of us. Let go of this dependence and you will find you are doing things for the right reason, to make *you* happier. It truly doesn't matter what people think. Their opinions are just passing thoughts and judgments in their minds and we are usually not even that important to them. So why should we place any significance on their opinions? We should really only care about the opinions of those who are close and dear to us.

This leads to a discussion of attitudes. Our attitude toward life in general, our dependence on other people's views of us, and our views toward our accomplishments guides the quality of our lives. We are unhappy, malcontent, or simply depressed if we fail to meet or surpass that which we expect of ourselves. Ironically, a component of human nature (part of our instinctive preprogramming) dictates that we never be satisfied with our current position in life, wherever that position may be. This is a valuable trait since it again motivates us to progress, to better ourselves and our positions no matter where we are in life.

Accordingly, we tend to behave much like a horse chasing a

carrot it can never reach since it's dangling in front of it from a stick attached to its back. We want, we set goals and dreams, we strive, we work, and often we find we arrive at success in our goal. But when we do, we immediately set a new goal since, once there, we cannot find satisfaction in what we already have. We must move up to the next level where we see others ahead of ourselves. Even after solid advancement, we tend to find a new "better" group by which we compare and judge ourselves against. The result of this is often a failure to ever enjoy our successes, however major or minor. This leads many to work feverishly all their lives only to find that when death is staring them in the face, they have regrets for "wasting" their lives chasing rainbows. When it was only our *gift of time* that really mattered.

We have to learn to enjoy the journey, not only the destination. Every day matters. Try and make every day count by using proper balance in life, a positive attitude and a sense of gratitude toward all the positives in life, to find joy in each day and to show appreciation for the time we have been gifted each day. Unfortunately, we tend to squander time today to have "more" tomorrow. Only when we are out of time do we realize that time itself was the only true valuable commodity.

The idea is not to say that we should not work hard or dream and strive to meet our dreams. It is to have the right attitude about it while we do it. To give proper balance and weight to everything positive in our lives, being grateful for all we have at each step of the way. To learn to value each day of our journey, not just the destination. Generally, reaching material wealth, fame, or status creates satisfaction in us. Yet, with the right attitude, we should experience satisfaction and happiness on the road to our successes. We should learn to appreciate and take joy in the small rewards and routines of our days. Family, friends, kids, pets, hobbies, entertainment, and just being alive. This is totally within our control. We can enjoy all these things as we strive for growth and success or we can largely ignore them as we spend our days in pure joyless effort. It depends on our ability to place proper weight on facets of our lives. Success isn't everything; our limited time here *is*. This is the essence of balance, attitude, and learning to properly appreciate all the positive things we take for granted in our lives. We'll discuss these further in later chapters.

CHAPTER 7

RIGHT AND WRONG

Looking at religion and religious belief with objectivity leads to a singular conclusion. Religion and its standards were created by man to control man. The origins of religion were probably not rooted in evil intentions. Maybe they were even inspired by spirituality. Most likely, they were initially created with the benign goal of creating harmony in coexistence for mankind.

Logically analyzing the content of the predominant rules and norms of religion leads to some highly probable conclusions. One, the rules were meant to solidify reverence for its object of worship and strict abidance to its wishes. And two, it was meant to promote the basic rules of peaceful coexistence where the dominance of physical strength gave way to rules of behavior that promoted reverence for the family and the mechanisms of progress.

These rules and laws are clearly in contrast with the realities of nature. Nature dictates survival of the fittest. That which takes survives. That which cannot protect itself, is consumed for the benefit of the strong. The laws and practices of religion are in general alien to the natural laws of our world. The concept of right and wrong are nonexistent in nature. Animal eats animal, especially the young and the weak. This is the law of nature. Compassion is reserved only for the offspring and family units where the objectives of continuation of the species and survival of the fittest of the species is served. As we look upon the natural world around us and extract the human religious influence, we find the world established by its Creator is void of the concepts of good and bad, right and wrong. These are concepts that are applicable to mankind alone. Maybe intentionally so.

We are told that the God of religion is benevolent, caring, compassionate, and ever diligent in watching over its creation. Reason and logic along with a simple, honest look at the world around us will clearly tell us that any Creator is simply uninterested in the protection of the weak and compassion toward the young. If we are to believe what we are told about the God defined by religion, we have to ask where is that God when children starve to death or are abused? Where is this God's compassion when his most faithful are stricken and suffering? If one looks at the realities of extremism in religion, another simple pattern reveals itself. All the heavily faithful people believe in the teachings of their childhood faith, with very rare exception. Almost none has chosen his or her religion; it has been chosen for them. How many extremists or deeply religious people do we know who applied their unbiased logic to all the different faiths and decided which was the right and just one to follow?

The bottom line is that hard faith and religious extremism stem from childhood brainwashing, something the human entity was designed to accept. Look at all the customs and practices of the various religions and belief systems. Each of us tends to think some other belief's customs and practices are ridiculous while our own are set forth by God and to be practiced and revered. One dances around a fire chanting, one prays against a wall for greater effect, and one circles an idol a certain number of times for acceptance. Who is right? Which procedure is actually the correct one to gain acceptance of

God? Why do we believe so vehemently in what we've been *told* is God's will?

In reality, the only protections we have to live relatively secure lives are the laws of man, whether religious or communal. No otherworldly intervention has ever exhibited itself as a compassionate helper of the needy and weak from above. When confronted with this apparent reality, most faithful followers of religion simply say, "God works in mysterious ways." Well, if we believe in a Creator that does not necessarily follow the description of the religious God, it is pretty apparent that this Creator does *not* work in "mysterious ways." Its "laws" are clear, its intentions are generally clear, and its direction is clear.

Every component of natural realities and behaviors on our earth is geared to the survival of life and the various species of life, *at all costs*. The simple conclusion evident from the facts strewn around us, is that we humans are here left to our own accord. We are given basic biological tools, intelligence, and an evolutionary mechanism to biologically adapt to our changing environment so we can assure the continuation of the species. It is as if we are an experiment to see where we will go and whether we will find the answers to our own existence.

Imagine one of those ant farms made with two plates of clear glass filled with sand and populated with ants. These were made so we could observe the ants' lives, their behavior and their reproduction. The ants do what they are compelled (programmed) to do. They dig tunnels and build chambers to raise their young. They forage for food and return to the nests at night. And as we watch them, they are oblivious to our observation. Their realm of scale is such that they are consumed with their own existence within their limited range of scale and we are too large for them to perceive and include in their realities.

Why do we watch them? We are curious and we are fascinated by the miniature world and its similarities to our own existence.

Can we also be a Creator's ant farm? Are we here as a test of our species? Are we a test of a certain newer design? Were the dinosaurs a failed version of an earthly experiment only to be replaced with a superior design? We have a large body of evidence going back over sixty-six million years depicting the world of the dinosaurs (which roamed the earth for almost 188 million years, the Mesozoic Era). And then we have good evidence of humanoids going back close to four million years. But there is not much in between that would evidence a progressive evolution from a smaller mammal leading to our early humanoid ancestors. And it is relatively clear neither mankind nor any large mammal existed during the Mesozoic Era. We seem to have appeared on the scene quite suddenly and with our advanced brains largely in place. Perhaps our Creator(s) invented a better version of carbon-based life and repopulated earth with it.

So, what is the "truth" about a possible Creator? It would seem that the Creator determined no right and wrong for its universe. We don't even know whether a potential Creator created the laws of physics or is also bound by them. Does the Creator work within the confines of its own existence in this universe or did it create the universe? We have no idea of the limitations created by the Creator versus the parameters the Creator was limited to.

How can we claim a universal "morality" when the very nature and realm of our known world is based on quite a different reality, the brutal laws of survival of the fittest? Life on our planet in large part has always depended upon the strong devouring the weak and helpless. It has depended on one species eating and therefore extinguishing the very life of the other. Survival of many species depends on this consumption of other life. Our morality has compassion for some animals, yet we kill a plethora of other animals (over 70 billion each year) without a second thought. Yes, we kill them, whether for sport or sustenance. It is convenient not to have to kill them personally; however, if we dine on them, we have killed them. We therefore only pacify ourselves with our "morality," which is purely a human notion. In any event, in our human realm, morality is a powerfully positive notion.

Compassion as an emotion is part of the human make up. However, it occupies the unique position of being available in direct proportion to how comfortable we happen to be. We are more compassionate if our basic needs are being met, but I assure you your disposition would be quite different if you and/or your children hadn't eaten for a week. As a society, as our needs have been more regularly provided for, we have become more compassionate and kinder. But the concept of right and wrong has been generally imposed upon us again with conceived logic, the rational goal of facilitating human co-habitation in communal settings. It makes perfect sense to be ruthless if we need to assure our survival, and it also makes perfect sense to become more concerned with co-existence, progress, and the "bigger picture" of our world when our survival is assured. We have been given this great range of behavior and emotion, from violent and ruthless to compassionate and kind. It is a range that is dependent on our survival instinct. In other words, we tend to be kinder and care more about what is "right" as we become more educated and advanced. Is this by design? Perhaps the design of mankind as implemented by an intelligent Creator.

However we look at it, it seems our lives are happier and more content as we progress. Our level of anger and propensity toward violence tends to subside as our compassion grows commensurate to our growth as a species. As we grow wiser and more learned, we have less need for the negative emotions that gave us an advantage in our more primitive states of humanity. Thus, we tend to become kinder and more tolerant, achieving a state more conducive toward more productive and more enjoyable lives. But some emotions persist through our more learned state. As an example, jealousy and greed continue to haunt us even when their usefulness has diminished. Emotions that negatively affect our level of happiness. This is where we can exert our own deliberate mental adjustments to better the quality of our lives.

Although the concepts of right and wrong may not be universal and may in reality be limited to humanity, these concepts are an important component and measure of our growth and advancement as a race. We have been given the ability to implement and live by our own full range of these concepts of right and wrong. We can live either way. But there certainly is a clear connection between the state of our scientific knowledge base and our movement toward the "right" on our scale. And also a clear connection between such movement to the righteous or enlightened state and our individual happiness.

CHAPTER 8

THE POWER OF OUR MINDS

One of the greatest powers we hold as individual human beings is the ability to materially affect our own mental state. We can achieve the remarkable by *adjusting* our own minds first and foremost. No one achieves anything that they do not *believe* they can achieve. To illustrate this reality, take the example of a person of average means and beginnings who truly believes that their life, like that of many generations of their family before them, will take a routine and specific course. They will ascend to a certain level in a career and make a certain amount of money and hope for a little more than that which can be expected from them. Can they go much further? Probably not. The limit the mind believes it cannot go beyond, becomes a very real limit. That perceived limit becomes our glass ceiling, so to speak. It is a limit only because *we believe* it is our limit.

Our perceived limits are generally effectuated in us by our life circumstances. Once we believe these limits, they are then truly limiting. For no limitation in life is more debilitating than our own subconscious mental beliefs. We can only do what deep inside we believe we *can* do. Believing we can do something is the greatest prerequisite and requirement for both action and achievement. Find the achiever and you will find a person who is either ignorant enough not to know limits or intelligent enough to know there *are* no limits.

It may sound metaphorical, but we mostly have no limits. Only those that our minds pretend are there. This is not a simple realization. It takes reflection and thought to really believe this. Some people are naturally blessed with an innate ability to know no limits. A vast majority of us, however, has built subconscious limitations for ourselves. But once this is realized and we work to eliminate the artificial ceilings, we begin to act quite differently. We begin to take the steps that are prevented by the lack of confidence dictated by limitations we believe we have. Many people will point to their difficult circumstances in life and swear by the validity of their own limitations. But because someone has a head start in their circumstances allowing them an easier time toward success, does not mean this premise of not having limits is invalid. At ground zero, you still have no limitations. There is no other way to account for the remarkable achievements of certain people who had no advantage. Their common denominator will always be two things: they knew no limits and they persevered. Both these qualities can be learned through the power we have to adjust our mental state. The nay-sayers, and there will be many, will claim that such mental functioning is inborn or inherited. Only you can be the ultimate proof for yourself. If you believe in a limit, it will *physically* be your limit. But if you believe the sky's the limit, you may not reach the sky, but you'll end up somewhere in between. That spot will be much higher than your perceived limit.

Our "comfort zones" are easy places to dwell in. Get out of your comfort zone. Challenge your glass ceilings. Go where you're apprehensive to go. Some of the greatest enduring memories in our lives are of the moments we challenged our fears and went out into the unknown. The exhilaration of facing our fears are some of our greatest times in our lives. Step out of your box.

THE GIFT OF FAILURE

Think about it and think about it deeply. If you can learn that you have only the limits of your own beliefs and nothing else, you have conquered your biggest obstacle to achievement and advancement. Your next obstacle will be the response to failure for, unless you are remarkably lucky, you *will* fail at some point. It's a terrifying word. "Failure." But it is all about how you perceive it. Your own attitude comes into play. Failure is often debilitating, but only because we let it be so. In reality, "failure" is simply a great learning experience. Much more so than even success. What you learn after a failed attempt is many times greater than what you learn when the attempt succeeds. There are many, many subtle reasons and alignments that result in success. When things fall into place, we don't always see or recognize these often hidden factors. But failure in an attempt usually accentuates the main reasons for its occurrence. We usually learn well from these and we are apt not to repeat their missteps. It makes us wiser and more likely to succeed.

Failure is only a steppingstone to success, but only if we allow ourselves to truly believe that. It builds a stronger and stronger foundation on which to then build a success. Our general reaction to failure is loss of confidence and therefore a regression to mental limitations. If after each failed step, no matter how many you encounter, you get up and forge forward with all your wounds and setbacks, you will find that each failure has taught you invaluable lessons and made you more likely to finally achieve your goals. With that mindset, each failure will only make you *stronger*. Lost all the

51

capital? Lost good will? *Find a way.* Almost all obstacles have a solution. They may be harder to overcome the second, third, or forth time around. But we can always find a way with creativity and effort. The more "failure," the merrier? Hard to digest, but ultimately true. If we let the initial failure crush us, where can we possibly go from there?

The fear of failure is one of the biggest obstacles to action and success. We need to learn that we don't need to avoid failure and we don't need to fear failure. Instead, we must acknowledge that failure is a necessary requisite of achieving our goals. With "failure," we learn more impactfully, we add to our foundational wisdom and preparedness for success, and we greatly reduce the chances of making mistakes in the same areas we have already erred. With "failure," certainly we will have setbacks, losses and disappointments. But if we keep forging forward with the confidence that, after however many "failures" it takes, we will ultimately reach our goal; and looking upon each set-back as a lesson learned, how can we *not* reach our goal? We can only truly never reach that which we have come to believe is impossible. Some rare things *are* impossible. But a vast majority of goals are well within our reach. This core concept is basically perseverance.

This is not to say that we should endeavor to fail. Naturally, if we can take successful steps, we want to strive to succeed each time we put forth an effort. The idea is not to be afraid of failure and to allow it to happen if it hits us after we have given it our best effort. The truth is that statistically, we will fail more often than we succeed. So, we need to learn to embrace it as a positive and build upon it. Use it as the truly empowering experience that it can be for us.

Perseverance is an interesting quality. Once we overcome our glass ceiling and truly believe we can accomplish great things, the only thing left to stop us is the self-defeating urge to surrender. How do you stop a person who won't surrender? Well, you really can't. They keep getting up and forging forward. So, they *will* eventually get to where they want to go. If they don't care how long it takes, how many failures they may encounter along the way, and what path they have to take, there's no stopping them. The most successful people I've known in my life have had this quality in common more than any other. They don't know how to quit. It's a state of mind. We can allow setbacks to defeat us or we can allow them to energize us in a renewed way to push toward getting to our goal. That state of mind is an attitude.

CHAPTER 9

ATTITUDE

We humans exist and function within our own distinct frame of reality, composed by our unique environmental and factual circumstances. The range of possibilities and circumstances in our lives is rather large. Some of us live at the far lower extreme of this range, which would be where subsistence and survival is the daily reality. Here, the mind is mostly concerned with where the next meal is to come from, and little else matters. The far other extreme is where the totality of human social and technological achievement is available to us, taken for granted, and the daily reality is purely competitive advancement. Here the mind is mostly concerned with status, achievement, and material gains.

We can function relatively well within the entirety of the spectrum between these two realms, which is vast. However, depending on where we live our lives within this wide spectrum, our perception of reality becomes very much limited to our own unique range within this overall spectrum of possible circumstances. In essence, we tend to be confined within our own limited range of the spectrum and we often lose our ability to consider, weigh, and assess the experiences of other people in other segments of this spectrum against our own. By way of example, a business failure that in the overall scheme of a person's existence may be somewhat of a minor consequence, may lead that individual to contemplate suicide. That person has become incapable of comparing his or her state to that of the mother whose problem is having to choose which of her two children to feed because she cannot feed both.

This habitual mental limitation is pervasive throughout our lives. We seem to be unable to place events we experience in life in a global perspective. We are slaves to our limited perspective created by our own unique circumstances in life in comparison to the larger spectrum of possibilities. In other words, we lose our conscious awareness of all the other very real areas of the full spectrum of circumstances. All those other possible realities start to fall completely outside our realm as we assess and ponder our own situation. We lose our ability to view them as real and possible circumstances of our own lives. And accordingly, we can no longer view them as a comparative base.

Where does attitude come into this picture? Our incredible human brain has an amazing ability that is infrequently utilized. That is the ability to deliberately adjust one's mental attitude and outlook. We all have different attitudes about everything in our lives, different perspectives. These variations in attitude make us view the same reality or circumstance in very different ways. And as we "see" things in these varied manners, this different viewpoint or attitude affects our internal and external reactions to our circumstance or issue in question. To adjust one's perspective requires one to step outside their natural boundaries within their own limited range amidst the larger spectrum of life. This can be done by realizing the global range as our perspective base. It is a mental adjustment of how we compare and evaluate our own circumstances. Looking at the extremes and comparing our own "mountains" may bring them back to the proverbial "mole hill" where they most frequently belong.

A "bad" attitude is generally its own punishment and, conversely, a "good" attitude is often its own reward as we are able, among many other benefits, to handle issues that confront us with less pain.

Attitude can be adjusted to rationalize our own responses to daily stimuli and events. Analyzing why we get angry at a certain event with a more global view may teach us that the anger is misplaced and only serves to hurt us and no one else. But this adjustment of attitude requires tremendous introspective analysis. We must analyze why we respond as we do, what is truly important, and what really requires any negativity or anxiety on our part at all. There are people who have mastered their attitude to an extent that almost nothing can cause them grief, anxiety, or depression. Everything is put in a global perspective and taken with the nominalism that it truly deserves in the larger picture of life. In a hundred years, what will it matter? If we learn to adjust our view so that we compare anything we deem "negative" to all the other possible negatives other people endure every day in the extremes, we will slowly learn to lessen our distress at our own predicaments.

Every minute of our lives is a precious gift. Nothing in this world can bring back lost time. It is a limited commodity and when it is gone, we are done on this earth. What should cause us to sour any given moment? Why allow anger, grief, depression, and angst to take over our precious time on this planet? What do we gain with these responses? Really nothing. By adjusting attitude to ultimately acknowledge that in the end we'll die and then nothing will have mattered other than the good moments we lived, we can better handle most of the curveballs thrown at us in life. As long as we don't unduly blow our issues and predicaments out of proportion, we can learn to handle almost any situation with a positive outlook and attitude.

As much as I believe in our ability to adjust our own mindsets,

I also acknowledge that there are many instances of chemical imbalances in the brain that create a various degree of serious ailments, including clinical depression. I don't mean to minimize the seriousness of these conditions. Often, they need medical remedies for real improvement. Although these thoughts are certainly not a cure for a serious medical condition, I still believe they can help as an adjunct to proper pharmaceutical intervention.

Are there things that hit us in life that are not so trivial to be minimalized with the proper attitude? Of course. Losing loved ones, serious illness, and many other issues are rightfully distressful and hard to minimalize. But even the grief of losing someone dear can be lessened with the proper attitude. Wouldn't they want you to be happy? Can their memory be a cause of good feelings? Can we temper the loss with the fact that they were a gift to us in life to begin with? Normally, we can still even lessen those times of great distress by not forgetting to consider how much worse things could be. The idea is to always give due consideration to what has not gone wrong or is relatively positive in our lives as we dwell on our woes. No matter what, we can learn to reduce negativity in our mindsets. We can learn to see our circumstances through a brighter lens.

Another thing to consider as we experience real challenges and negative events in our lives that we really have no control over, is the fact that often these events are potentially precursors to a positive occurrence in our lives. It's certainly difficult for us to imagine any good coming from what we deem a tragedy at the moment. But it does often happen that what we perceive as a great negative ends up leading to something positive. A simple example may be getting fired from a job, a terrible experience. But maybe the fact of being out of that job led to another opportunity that was a huge positive: another job that would never had presented itself if we were happily continuing on in the old job. It happens more often than you might think. That's not to say that it will always happen. But it's another thing we can believe in as a possibility to lessen the negative impact of an event. It's the proverbial belief of a silver lining to a dark cloud.

An event that made me aware of this possible silver lining and the role of attitude in actually helping that silver lining come to fruition happened to my closest and dearest friend, Rob. A person I have learned from greatly in life. Rob lived on his family ranch in the mountains of Santa Barbara. Everything he possessed was on that ranch. A wildfire swept the mountains of Santa Barbara that year and destroyed everything in its path, including the ranch. Nothing remained but a smoldering patch of dirt and melted components of glass and vehicles. I stood with him at the top of the hill surveying the damage, feeling terrible for my friend. What he said next confounded me. He said, "This is good, this is a fresh start. I'm going to build it back better than it was." How could he see anything positive in that dark moment? He didn't have a home, a vehicle, nor even clothes to wear. Two years later, he had a far superior property looking better than it ever had. His attitude probably contributed to his success in rebuilding a better property. But more importantly, it avoided suffering in the aftermath which in the end turned out to be needless. There is some level of richness in almost everything, even in situations that may seem terribly negative. We just need to have the "vision" to see that richness.

It all begins with our attitude. We can make a mountain out of a molehill with attitude and we can make a molehill out of a mountain with attitude. We each have our own unique and individual ability to create the appropriate attitude adjustments in ourselves. It is a power we have, but seldom use. It takes a lot of practice and conscious effort to make these adjustments to our attitude. But in the long run, we can make it happen, if only we try. Too few even try.

CHAPTER 10

GRATITUDE

Over the many centuries of our existence as a race, through our increasing knowledge and learning, we have made life easier and easier for ourselves. Spending our days foraging and hunting for subsistence gave way to having easy access to three meals a day without any need to worry about hunger. Step by step we have gained organization, specialization, and cooperation so that our lives became less about survival and more about growth and gain. But again, due to our human nature, we have slowly lost touch with the hardships we historically have faced. Our human condition dictates that we pocket the benefits of our progress while we find new worry about what more there is to gain.

We worry about what we don't have and grieve for what could have been or could be. In this process, we have lost an immense sense of gratification: the gratitude for all we *have* gained and all we take for granted. We have forgotten how hard life can be and how hard it once was. What we have really lost in this is the joy and satisfaction of our progress. We have lost thankfulness. We have forgotten to take the time to reflect upon all that is positive, all the negative that is no longer our bane, and all the good that surrounds us.

Gratitude brings a tremendous reward of its own. If we take a few moments every day, maybe when we awake or maybe before we fall asleep, to think about all the good people in our lives, friends, family, mates, pets, all those we love, the meals we enjoy regularly and easily, the roof over our heads, the possessions we hold, the health we harbor, the good times we experience down to the beauty of the day we have just lived or are about to live through, and to give thanks for these blessings, we will find a joy that has been lost. And most importantly, we should acknowledge and appreciate the fact that we are alive.

We are here on earth at this moment in time, walking the world with our contemporaries and experiencing our gift of life and our gift of time. We and everyone else here today will be gone 120 years from now. We are a temporary link in the chain of humanity exactly like all the others who have lived before us, lived their time, and are now gone. Just like them, so too shall we be gone one day and the world will be inhabited by a whole new generational link in the chain.

All it takes is a few minutes of reflection to arrive at a true sense of positive gratitude. Try it as an experiment. Take thirty seconds every day to think of all the positive, beautiful, and rich elements of the circumstances in your life and give thanks for those things. Try to make a list of every positive thing you can imagine down to the smallest thing like a sunset you just may have experienced. Soon you will find that you have a long list. There is so much to be thankful for. Even if there is plenty of grief in our lives, there is still room for gratitude. It could always be worse. Always. If we truly feel the gratitude, it will eventually give way to a sense of euphoria and happiness. Over time, we will find we are happier people in general. Able to see what we had become blind to. Able to appreciate the simple pleasures, wonders, and benefits we live with and we take for granted. We start to balance the scale of negativity with true awareness of the other side of the scale. All by simply giving thought to what is *real*. Giving thought to what is truly positive that we have forgotten to add to the right side of the scale as we weigh the good and bad in our lives.

So, however we deal with the negatives, if we only recall and appreciate all that is right and all the positive elements in our lives, including simply being alive, the fact that this is a lopsided equation will become more and more apparent to us, lessening our distress over the negative experiences.

I believe that a vast majority of people have many more multiple times the good and positives in their lives than they have painful challenges. If we only learn to open our eyes more regularly to the positives we take for granted, to acknowledge all the good in our lives, we will see how blessed we truly are. Keep in mind, there will *always* be challenges in our lives. If we let these less than desirable occurrences and issues ruin our days, when will we be able to experience happiness? We need to be able to counter all our challenges with the acknowledgement of the many, many positives in our lives. Even the most minute positive element.

Try lying in silence to make your list and grant proper weight to all the positive factors in your life. Then try and make a habit of it, doing it every day. Saying your thanks to whomever or whatever you feel is responsible for all the goodness. Your god, the spirits, the universe, the collective consciousness, your ancestors, whatever. And letting it sink in how much is in your life that is truly positive. And fully acknowledging how bad things *could* be. Even if there are great challenges and stresses in your life, acknowledge the balance between the good versus the negative. Feel gratitude for the good and positive around you. Make your mental list and give weight to *each and every* positive component in your world. Truly feel the joy of these positive elements. See what happens.

In most people's circumstances in their lives, there is a great more good and positive than negative realities at any given time. So, let's give more gratitude for the good circumstances we have than lament what we are missing. Give proper acknowledgement and weight to all the good in your life.

CHAPTER 11

BALANCE

The concept of balance is in direct contrast with an enduring human quality, polarization. We tend to be black or white about most of our options in life. We often tend to pick an ideology and to follow its views without much regard for the logic and rationale of the opposing side's point of view. In our personal allocation of our energies and in our character traits, we also often tend toward the extremes. For many of us, we either love to work to or we hate it, we are either very conservative or liberal, we are affectionate or cold, introverted or extroverted. Balance in our life is not naturally there and must come with deliberate effort. It does not come naturally to almost anyone. We must strive to find happy mediums within our lives. For example, a life where one works themselves to death is probably as wasted as one where there is no accomplishment or satisfaction related to work. Balance is finding the median road, being able to moderate our views and our own characters toward the areas where we do not readily identify.

To find the balance or the middle range of any aspect of our lives leads to happier more fruitful lives. Why is this? First, the extremist assessment and view of any situation tends to deny any credibility to opposing views and accordingly is often simply wrong. Not entirely wrong, but wrong in its isolated extreme point of view. Most often, in a variety of issues, there is no clear and simple right and wrong.

Take the incendiary issue of abortion. Very polarized, highly emotional. At the extremes, we are inflexible, we are angry, and we *fight*. An uncomfortable disposition. But is the extreme view correct, in either direction? Can we say a healthy growing human being in the uterus is absolutely subject to termination even when it could possibly survive outside the womb? Or can we really dictate to a woman that she *must* become a mother when she may not be ready or have the proper resources to care for a child, potentially ruining her life, hopes, and dreams? Especially if that pregnancy can be terminated early on at a time when developmentally, the fetus has no resemblance to a human being and cannot survive outside the womb? Good questions. No clear answer. Debatable both ways. So why are we so fanatic about this issue to the point where we can't say, as painful as it may be, that there's a possible common ground middle point that addresses the majority of each point of view?

Both sides have dramatically valid points. Existing in the extreme is uncomfortable. We are bitter and incensed by the arguments of our opponents. That brings with it a certain type of misery. Anger is a stressful and uncomfortable emotion. When we are angry, we are in fight mode. Adrenalin is flowing, muscles tighten, and all mental capacity is dedicated to battle. But if we're willing to find that balance in our view, to respect what the other point of view is and to consider its issues, we can find a middle ground and we will also find a happier, less angry state of being simply because we are not at the extreme. Finding empathy toward other people's beliefs and points of view is actually enlightening and a relief to our stress levels.

The second is that a balance in both how we think and how we act creates equilibrium. Our human lives are consumed with communal interactions and the exercise of our great range of emotions. Within our realm, is the ability to comprehend certain things by comparison. It is hard for us to fathom the concept of "good" if we have no reference to "bad." How do we define light if we don't know darkness? Can we know the meaning of "peace and calmness" if we don't know it's opposite, "hysteria and chaos"? Without this comparative range within which to define things in our lives, there would be less range in our existences. Maybe we'd be more like ants or fish, systematically going through a programmed life with limited choices. This concept has been around for hundreds of years. What is relatively apparent is that we feel the most contentment at the central parts of these ranges. We thrive in the middle, so to speak. This applies to almost any condition or range of emotions we experience in our lives. Balance is twofold. It is balancing various components in our lives and it is also finding the "sweet spot" center of our emotional and physical wellbeing.

Any time we are predisposed with a specific facet of our lives, it takes over our focus, usually at a cost of other areas that then get ignored or underplayed. This imbalance can sometimes have a positive effect as well, such as if we are completely preoccupied with work and success. But even though we may do well financially, is it worth the cost of finding time to enjoy our lives in other ways? Travel, time with family and friends, hobbies, or the outdoors? Is it not a more satisfying life to have balance in all these areas, sacrificing none to the other? Balance in our life creates harmony and spreads our attention in a manner that delivers more and varied satisfaction. Balance in our thinking and in our expenditure of our time and energies in all areas of our lives brings less stress and greater happiness.

The same is true for almost every other aspect of our lives. Work, play, socializing, sex, even fun. When we create a balanced level of anything in our lives, we will find a happier existence. If you play all day, assuming you can afford to do so, you will miss out on the great satisfactions that come from hard work and achievement.

One incredibly important part of balance in our lives is the maintenance of some level of physical activity. In our modern lives, it is easy to ignore this element as much of our daily physical labor has become mechanized. Exercise is immensely important for mental health and mood as well as for the body itself. This doesn't require a large amount of activity. Even a small effort to exercise a few times a week is very rewarding. Each of us has to settle on a level that meets our physical ability dependent on age and health. For some a brisk walk and for others maybe an hour of aerobic exercise to elevate the heart rate. But without a balanced amount of exercise, the body and the mind begin to lose function and durability.

Balance is a skill that if mastered, can bring tremendous quality to our lives. In each and every situation we may find ourselves, we can improve on the balance. Simply put, it is a conscious effort of trying to moderate to the center. To become well rounded and proportionate in our thinking, our attitudes, our values, our character, and our actions.

The last three topics discussed above, attitude, gratitude, and balance are some of the most important tools we can use to better our own lives and achieve more fulfillment and happiness. If you take nothing else from these writings, consider these three concepts carefully. They are real assets to living better and happier lives.

CHAPTER 12

HAPPINESS

One of the key elements to our happiness is to truly understand the human condition, as imposed upon us, both by our preprogramming prior to birth (our natural instincts) and by the influences in our formative years, and to then work to adjust our own mindset with rational decision making. We need to stand outside our bubble of perception and look at ourselves from the outside. We need to understand how we are programmed, the ranges we've been given, and the likely reasons for certain aspects of our biological programming. Once we understand these, and accept their function, we can start to find the paths most conducive to true contentment and happiness.

The more we master some of the elements of our thinking, which we have previously discussed, the more likely we are to experience true happiness. We need to learn to control our minds, emotions and thought processes, to be released from our instinctive programming where that programming is not conducive to our happiness. Attitude, balance, gratitude and our own dependence on other people's opinions are some of the mental elements we have the power to adjust and modify. Doing so is not a menial task. It takes time, effort, and deliberate thought and consideration. But over time, we can slowly adjust these components of our internal thoughts and find ourselves more content and happy on a daily basis.

We are put on this earth as biological machines with a certain level of intelligence and a myriad of emotions. This is our core condition, and then we have our free will. We are programmed as we program our machines, but we can affect and modify our own programming. The emotions within us are intertwined with our intelligence and a part of our programmed design. Is the realm of emotion universal? Does our Creator feel emotions? The same as ours or possibly others unknown to us? We certainly don't have a clue. But what is relatively apparent is that our emotions guide us in life and as we gain knowledge, the reliance on emotions is lessened. It is also relatively clear that even romantic love is a chemically induced, programmed emotion in us just as any other emotion. Evidence of this is the lack of romantic love toward the opposite sex in a child. This particular emotion almost always presents itself in adolescence when many chemical and hormonal changes are taking place in the body. It begins when chemicals in the brain are released in conformance with timed (it starts at a certain age) programming within the brain.

Emotions have been built into us to help the species flourish without reliance on our own thought processes to compel us into action. For example, we feel fiercely protective of our offspring, instinctively. And we anger and strengthen with adrenaline with the appearance of a perceived threat. Another more subtle example is our tendency to worry and be anxious about uncertainties. These emotional reactions were especially beneficial with the limited "raw" human mind, unlearned and unrefined. As we learn more, we tend to use logic to make our decisions and guide our behavior versus relying on our primal emotions. So, it would at least seem that emotions within us are, as much of our instinctive behavior (programming) is, elements to guide our survival and growth until we are "smart" enough to operate on factual knowledge and intelligence. Thus, learning to master our emotions with our logic and rational thinking is a critical component of our individual progress and contentment.

It would seem that the Creator programmed us with these primal emotions to include a great range within each type of emotion. The human condition is that we are primarily greedy, but we have great capacity for generosity. We are often hateful, but capable of great love. We are easy to anger, but we can feel great joy and happiness. We can be vicious and violent, but also compassionate and caring. We all feel the full range of each emotional set, but we each tend to adapt to certain smaller ranges within the larger total range of an emotion. This is partly inherent to our natural individual makeup but largely dependent on environmental influences and our level of learning. And interestingly enough, it also seems that the more we acquire knowledge and apply our intelligence, we tend to shift our behavior in the emotional ranges toward the "positive" side. We are kinder, more accepting and more compassionate. As our brains are equipped with the tools of learning and a curiosity to know, it would seem the natural order or the Creator's intent may have been to enhance human survival at the less "intelligent" stages versus giving man the ability to experience peace and harmony when he was sophisticated enough to ensure his survival with his knowledge.

So, what does this have to do with happiness? It seems happiness is more manifest as we tend to shift toward the "positive" end of our emotional scales. We are happier when we are kind and giving. We are happier when we have serenity and not anger. We are happier when we accept others and don't feel hatred. Part of learning to be happier in life is also learning to use our knowledge and intelligence to dull our propensity toward the more primal, survival-based end of our emotional spectrum.

Again, we can't simply think this into existence. It takes thoughtful effort and work to become more aware of our own emotional response at any given moment and to put them into check. It takes thoughtful effort and work to ascertain why we are feeling negative feelings and to reflect on the nature of our programming and how we have the power to modify how we are feeling through rationalization. For example, when we feel hatred toward another, it rarely does much harm to the target of that hate. But it causes all kinds of damage to us. So why hate? Why allow a primal reaction to harm ourselves? Why not *let things go* in the pursuit of peacefulness and a happier existence? We absolutely have the power to change our programmed emotional response.

Worry is another damaging and relatively useless emotion that prevents a happier mental state. We worry because we *anticipate* possible negative events. We can still think ahead and try and prevent these negative events, but we should learn to let go of the worry. It does nothing to stop what can happen. It only makes us suffer even if the negative event never comes to fruition. We can learn to let go of the worrying and allow the negative feelings to effect us only in the event something bad actually happens.

But if there's a true secret to happiness, it resides in our capacity for unconditional love. It's definitely a misnomer as no love is absolutely unconditional. But some love takes a relatively pure form that doesn't have much expectation for anything in return. It is a true, deep and selfless love of another person (or animal). Family, mates, and friends are all people we tend to love. But the connection to happiness is not so much about volume as it is about quality in our relationships.

We humans are social animals. We thrive amongst our peers and we perish in isolation. But what kicks us a few steps up the happiness scale are the relationships we nurture that end up being truly deep and mostly unconditional love, such as the love we feel for a child, a parent, a soulmate, or a best friend. It is a love that is so meaningful and mutual that it literally releases large quantities of dopamine in our brains when we are around these people. And as we are essentially ultra-sophisticated and chemically driven machines, our emotions are largely dependent on the brain chemicals that make us happy.

Our true treasures in life, therefore, have to be "those" people in our lives. The ones we love unconditionally, and we are loved by unconditionally. The real measure of a rich person in my mind is the number of these people in their lives and the depth of those relationships, not dollars in an account. Don't get me wrong. Money is a wonderful thing. It can bring its own contribution to happiness. But it does not equate to happiness. If you think so, just look at the number of enormously wealthy people who were and are chronically unhappy. I know a ton of them. And the happiest people I've known in my life are the ones with the best strong and deep relationships and the right attitudes in their lives. If you have someone in your life who would drop everything to be there for you in times of trouble, hang on to that person for dear life and be the best friend you can be to that person. And learn to truly appreciate what those people mean to you in your life. They are your keys to a happier existence.

CHAPTER 13

LOGIC AND LOGICAL DESIGN

Logic is the incredibly powerful tool that provides the ability to take each step required to arrive at scientific discovery. In the world we live in, things don't just happen. Things happen for a reason. There is a logical explanation for almost everything we see in nature. Our acquisition of knowledge over the many decades has given us more and more insight into the reasons things are the way they are.

Without our current level of knowledge, we were only able to explain many of the things we experienced in nature with mysticism and conjecture. Imagine the relatively raw mind of a cave dweller seeing a rainbow for the first time. How could he explain it without conjuring up myth? The simple realization of cause and effect would make this person need an explanation. Without the science to give an adequate explanation, the mind looks for answers elsewhere. When a logical path is not presented, our human minds tend to believe the most fascinating and "magical" explanation. Hence, throughout history, mankind has created stories and mythology to explain what it could not with logic.

Various religious and cultural beliefs are examples of this broad body of mostly baseless mythology. As we have gained more factual knowledge through science and rational analysis, we have slowly discredited most of the myths of old. As scientific explanation provides more and more answers to the wonderment around us, we rely less on old, foundationless explanations taught throughout prior generations. In short, logic replaces myth as a way to understand our world.

We now understand how we can create great things with logical designs. We have created our own collection of machines, large and small. That has given us a better ability to look at nature's designs and better appreciate the massive intelligence required behind some of its workings. We have come to understand and appreciate the rule of logic.

We as humans are bound by the natural constraints of the structure and function of our physical mind. We are subject to our emotional makeup, instinctive needs, and programmed reactions. The world around us, however, largely functions on the principals of logic and order. The laws of physics and chemistry primarily determine the workings of our earthly world, our very bodies, and a large part of our perceivable universe. As mankind has gained more and more understanding of this logical world, we have relied less and less on mysticism and myth to explain the incredible world around us.

However, in our greatly accelerated acquisition of scientific knowledge over the last two centuries, perhaps we have come to a certain arrogance of knowledge. We collectively seem to believe that we have advanced and gained understanding of our universe far more than is warranted. We often fail to acknowledge how very little we know even with how far we have come in science. There is just so much more yet to discover and such a great deal more we can learn and understand. Accordingly, we have tried to answer questions of creation and the cosmos by way of our current state of knowledge. We have, woefully inadequately, tried to explain the origin and extent of the universe as well as the circumstances of our own creation. As we further learn about laws governing the universe, we may be able to answer some of these elusive questions, although we may never be able to fully comprehend the expanse of knowledge binding our universe.

These limitations have stared us in the face from the beginnings of mathematical reasoning. A prime example of this is the concept of infinity. We cannot explain infinity, nor can we truly understand it. Like a primate who may demonstrate a degree of rudimentary logic yet cannot be expected to understand quantum mechanics because of the physical limitations of its brain, we too are bound by certain limitations we simply cannot surpass. Our greatest minds have not been able to begin to explain these concepts, which must play into the universal answers we seek.

We strive to explain the limits of the universe by suggesting it is still growing. What is it growing into? What's behind and around it? Taken literally, the concept of infinity means we must first traverse one-half a given distance and then again, one-half of the remaining distance, and so on. So how do we ever get from point A to point B? If the half distance goes on indefinitely, we technically can't reach our destination. It never stops; we can always cut a given distance in two. The point is, infinity doesn't work in our practical world. It's a concept beyond our comprehension. Time plays into infinity. It does not stop like counting cannot stop. Yet every finite thing is made finite by its limit in time.

We simply cannot fathom the limitless. Everything we know has a limit. If we cannot understand that one concept, can we hope to understand our Creator, our purpose, life, creation itself? No one knows, but we like to pretend like we do. We need to fully acknowledge our limitations. As much as we've learned, there is so much more we don't know, maybe so much more we *can't* know. This incredible world we live in on our magical planet has so many fascinating secrets from its microscopic makeup of a cell that supports the entire larger species of the animal kingdom, to the intricate balance of all its lifeforms and ecological systems. With the entirety of life being adapted to the physical world through the programs and workings of that single cell. In reality, we know very little of what is visible to us today, let alone what further knowledge is out in our universe that we have no current way of perceiving.

We were put on this earth with no knowledge built into our brains. We have instinctive programming and we have been given our emotional ranges. And most importantly, we were given intelligence and the capacity to rationalize and learn. Through our slow growth in knowledge, we have come to build great things. We have built ships, skyscrapers, and electronic devices, and we have propelled ourselves to the moon and back. All this was done by learning science and extracting raw elements from our basic earthen surroundings.

Like our miracle little cell, which has had that technology for millions of years, we have come to learn to take elements from the earth, modify and purify them with scientific processes, and then build useful items and machines through logical design. It has taken us millions of years to get to the point we are at today. And with all our logical inventions and designs (we have put robots on Mars) we can't yet understand many fundamental mechanisms and the overall logical design inherent within our own cells and beings.

Logic is the foundation of everything we've built to date. Not faith, not emotions and not accident. Our emotions and our faith may compel us to move forward, but only logic has served to truly build and advance us to where we are today. Our "creativity" in building and advancing has been a usage of logic in design. And therefore, it is logic we must apply to answer the questions of our existence and of our universe. We need to learn to extract emotion and our instinctive programming from our quest in this regard. When we look at the logic applied to our own inventions and also look at the scale of logic incorporated into our biological beings, it becomes pretty clear we are not the only conveyors of logic in this universe. There is so much logic and science well beyond our current state of knowledge. We all must now acknowledge the need to move to more purely logical thinking as we continue to grow and advance our human race.

CHAPTER 14

SCALE

In the quest for knowledge of our earthly world and the universe surrounding it, we have been and are extremely limited by our viewpoint within the scale of size. There are the "small" things we cannot see and the very "large" that overwhelm us that we also cannot readily "see". We have just begun to break out of our natural limitations with the notion of size and evaluate the world with reference to a much larger spectrum. We are now more able to explore the infinitesimally small, nuclear components that make up everything larger. If we could see further into the smaller components, what else would we find? Other universes, possibly? Could infinity be a circle or sphere where infinity outbound coincides with infinity inbound? Is there a connection between infinitesimally small and large?

In the human realm, we live in a certain range of scale in the spectrum of "size." On one end is the infinitesimally small. We can now see far into this end with electron microscopes and other instruments. But we still stop short. Imagine if we were the size of an atom and our perspective could go smaller from there. How much smaller can we go? Remember, anything and everything can be cut in half, endlessly. On the other end of the scale is the infinitesimally large. Traveling at the speed of light (186,000 miles per second), we could travel for *millions* of years and pass planets, galaxies and stars in the billions, a "size" that our minds can't readily grasp. We can pass planets that dwarf the earth as an elephant dwarfs a grain of sand.

Somewhere in between is a range of size that is "tangible" to humans and human perception. We can largely perceive a limited range of the size scale surrounding the regions of our own size. It is difficult for us to readily grasp much beyond this limited scale. We can handle, manipulate, and comprehend from a small grain of sand to a large manmade building. But it becomes difficult to truly understand the larger scale of our planet and the universe and so we use models and renderings to help us. Light-years of distance are relatively incomprehensible to us. And then we can also go the other direction, from the little flea we can see under a magnifying glass to a whole world of living creatures we cannot see with our naked eyes. And further down to the atoms and molecules that are an equal magnitude of size difference as the universe is to our earth. And how far can we go? What even smaller elements make up the atoms and the molecules?

This is the realm of "scale." With our current instruments designed to give our naked eye access to more of the scale in each direction, we can see worlds previously unknown to us. Outside of that expanded range, we can only use our imaginations to "see" both directions and how massively large and infinitesimally small the ends of the scale can be. But we humans do, for all practical reasons and outside our scientific knowledge, only exist in our own limited section of the scale of "size." And it is difficult for our minds to truly comprehend the extreme ranges of the scale of size.

Is there an existence or a being that transcends this scale? If we have a Creator, can it function and readily perceive at all levels of this scale, unlike our own limited range? Its ability to operate in a much, much larger section of scale would be unquestioned as life is built within a range that goes far beyond our conscious awareness of size. Could a possible Creator or Creators exist at the extremely small end of the scale, building "massive" beings out of their inventions? The cell and all its functions operate on an infinitesimally small size compared to some of the larger lifeforms they make up, like a whale. Many trillions of cells have to join to make such lifeforms. And then these cells have components and capabilities that probably go down an equal percentage in the "smaller" direction. Imagine the cell being the size of the whale and the cell's own internal functional components (in the thousands) being the respective size of the cell to us.

Conversely, if we could make ourselves small enough to put the cell in front of us in the size of a plate, imagine what size our own cells would then become. Imagine how much easier it would be to discover the secrets of our own cells if their functionality was readily visible to us. If our own scale of perception allowed us to readily look into the many components and operations of the cell, we may be many decades ahead in our knowledge derived from the existing realities of biological life. Many of our recent discoveries have occurred simply because we have developed new instrumentation that allows us to transcend our limitations in size and scale and to peer into the workings of microscopic life.

Adding to the plethora of our human limitations is our limited range in the spectrum of scale. We are slowly gaining on this limitation as we learn of the great distances of the universe and the corresponding atomic distances going inward toward the minute. But we still cannot comprehend the concept of infinite scale and range, which is somehow a part of universal existence. It seems pretty clear that as intelligence and knowledge increase, the range of scale within which our minds can function and process concepts, increases. It is also relatively apparent that a Creator responsible for the blueprint of life on earth would have tremendous ability to transcend our limited scale. Life has been designed with full "vision" into the microscopic and further to the atomic levels of scale all the way to the largest mammals living on earth. A massive range. It is also highly likely that a Creator's insight into scale transcends into the largest expanses in the space of the universe.

CHAPTER 15

OUR PERCEPTION OF TIME

We all consciously know we will die one day. This knowledge is embedded in our logical thinking mind, derived from fact and reality. However, there is a more powerful and instinctive belief deeply hidden in our sub-conscious mind that harbors no doubt that we, individually, are immortal. We, our mind, perceives the world, so how can the world exist without our mind? And even though our logical mind very clearly admits our mortality, we tend to live our lives like we are immortals. Our actions are often based on the subconscious belief that we will always be around and not eventually die.

This subconscious notion is a powerful one. In our lives, we experience others who become very sick. Some die of their illnesses and some succumb to accidents. But even as we acknowledge rationally that it could happen to us, deep down there is a belief that it cannot. "It won't happen to me" may not be spoken often, but it is what our psyche believes. This subconscious belief leads to a perception of endless time. If we truly and deeply accepted that our lives are simply equal to a finite number of minutes and seconds, we would live our lives differently. Why does youth waste its precious time? Because the young, much more so than older people, innately believe their time on earth is endless. Only when it is almost gone do we tend to realize how finite it truly *was*. We get better and better at accepting our finality as we grow older, but the persistent underlying *subconscious* belief makes us feel immortal even to our deathbed.

The trick is not to simply admit we are mortal. We clearly already do that. It is to challenge the sub-conscious mind to grasp that time is limited for us. It is a finite gift. And therefore, it must be used wisely and, to the maximum extent possible, to give us happiness and pleasure *in the present*.

We build for the future and so we must as planning and building is what delivers results and achievements. However, too many of us only build for the future on the expectation that nothing is lost if we don't "live" today, for there is always tomorrow. The bad news is, there is not always tomorrow. Not only are we finite, but we must steer through a course of life's natural and unnatural risks that may take us at any moment. If we do not believe at our core that we are mortal, we certainly cannot believe that terminal illness can end *us*. We do fear death, but we fear it mostly instantly, at the current moment of great danger. This, as all of our instinctive programming, serves a purpose: it makes us avoid danger and therefore increases our chances of survival. We fear death as a survival instinct. But there is also a primal need *not* to accept it subconsciously so we can continue building and progressing in life without feeling it is all for naught.

Our senses of depression and hopelessness would be greatly enhanced in us if we did not have this innate "feel" of immortality. But we can truly serve ourselves by letting that surface knowledge of our eventual demise penetrate deep into our psyche so our subconscious also accepts the fact of our finality and our limited gift of time. Once we accept it deeply and accept the limits of our gift of time in this world, we will be motivated to enjoy life more fully each day. We will focus energy on living well and pleasurably *now* using proper values and attitudes. We will be more apt to embrace life with less hesitation and fear and take active steps now rather than later to reach goals that may bring us joy. We will "do" in the immediate time frame if we take away our notion of endless time. With the deep realization that our time is finite, we will be less likely to leave things we want to do till tomorrow. That's where it begins to suffocate our ability to enjoy today the way it should be enjoyed. With a sense of immortality, we can end up being relatively sedentary all our lives.

Time is an interesting notion. It's like a continuing piece of magnetic tape. You can only see or hear what's on it exactly at the point the tape is going by the reader head. But with time, you can't rewind it, not even for a second. It moves forward relentlessly, pausing for nothing and no one. Yes, we are learning that time and space can bend and shift. But not in our human realm. We have the moment and then the moment is gone. The only real life we have is in this present moment. What we do in this present moment, both in planning and in actions, dictates the framework of the future. So, our existence is really only in the present moment. The point is, what are you doing in your moment?

Each moment is part of your gift of time that is being spent regardless of what you do with it. Certainly, we should invest portions of our moments in a variety of work, progress, learning, planning, socializing, and all the other ways we spend our time. But regardless of what you are doing, make sure your moment is a happy one. Almost anything we do can be made better by the general attitudes we carry in our lives overall. Making the moments we spend on anything that makes us happy makes them a good investment. With adjustments in our attitudes and our propensity to take action on our desires, we can make those moments a better use of our time. And it is absolutely within our own power to adjust our own thinking to make the majority of our moments enjoyable, no matter what we're doing.

CHAPTER 16

SPIRITUALITY

What is spirituality? In my mind, it is simply a belief that there is more to life and existence than we as mortals are able to perceive. It gives a certain acceptance and credence to unknown forces in our universe and in our lives with a leaning toward positivity and "goodness." We all harbor some spirituality even if we are strongly religious people. There certainly is spirituality in religiousness. It is again part of the human condition to be spiritual. We need to believe in something more than what is before our eyes. We all feel that there is more to life than what we are able to observe and understand.

The difference between being religious and spiritual is that religious people have applied their "need to believe" to a preset belief system and school of thought whereas the spiritual person is more apt to accept the "I don't know" philosophy and apply their belief to embrace the "unknown" while leaving it relatively unknown. Accordingly, spiritual people are less apt to preach about their beliefs and less apt to judge or condemn others for their beliefs.

Becoming more educated and "worldly" doesn't mean we have to give up on our sense of spirituality. In fact, I believe we tend to move from adherence to religion more toward spirituality as we become more knowledgeable and advanced. Spirituality is certainly a good thing. It is a positive element in our lives as long as it's not exclusionary and we allow others to believe what they believe. It is the essence of non-judgment. Live and let live. And by avoiding the anger and hatred toward others, we lead better and happier lives ourselves.

Again, the concepts of right and wrong are not necessarily "natural." There is no indication that they have been set forth by our Creator. Nature operates with complete disregard for this concept. For the most part, when religion advertises right and wrong, it is serving its age-old dual purpose of peaceful human cohabitation and the more sinister goal of controlling the masses. Arguably, religion's most fascinating creation is the concept of heaven and hell. Reward or punishment. Act as we say and you will be rewarded in eternity. Do what we prohibit and you will be punished for eternity. With our great need to believe, we are apt to easily accept these concepts.

Is there really a heaven and hell? I don't know. But I certainly don't think so. The evidence in nature shows an entirely different story. Is there life after death? Again, I don't know. Nobody does. But there is a great body of research that shows a commonality in the experience of death amongst those who have been clinically dead and have been revived back to life. They see a bright light, experience serenity and joy, and often see passed-on loved ones beckoning them forward to the light. Is this evidence of an after-life? Or is this a result of a built-in programming in our brain to give us a last bit of solace and peace as we go into oblivion? Will our consciousness survive our biological death? I certainly don't know. But as we progress forward in our knowledge, especially with creating artificial intelligence that can operate similar to the human brain, we will learn more about the realities of consciousness and its possible existence outside our bodies and in other mediums unknown to us today.

Spirituality is clearly a positive attribute. But is it that religion is wrong and it's God should not be worshiped? These views may seem to suggest that, but in reality, religion and faith in God serves us well. It accounts for most of us fearing doing wrong to each other, it promotes harmonious living (at least within its own religion) and it satisfies our very primal need to believe in a greater force, someone watching over us in our most trying times, our security blanket. These are all provided by faith, whatever the religion may be. Faith as a whole is a good thing. It is the spiritual component of religion. The belief in a logical Creator can be faith, belief in science can be faith, in Jesus, Allah or Moses, Buddha or God. Whatever we choose to call it, we feel warmth in knowing we can speak to it. We take comfort in believing it is our protector.

Real or not, each of us benefits greatly by believing or having faith in something greater than our own humankind. This faith creates internal peacefulness and harmony within societies. It promotes the very basic core of the survival of our species, the family. However we acquire this faith, either by accepting the preaching and teachings of others or by our own logical opinion-forming processes, there is nothing negative about our personal faith. It is a problem when this faith starts to manifest itself as a vehicle for oppressing the faith and beliefs of others. It is a problem when this faith finds leadership that is convinced that the faith is a source of power and must be imposed upon others, by promotion or by force. It is a problem when it becomes a tool to promote hatred of non-devotees. It is also a problem when it dictates and promotes prejudice against particular types of people within the religion itself.

We have created the concept of right and wrong to control our own behavior. Through the tremendous power of religion, which basically feeds on the individual's faith, we have been given "rights" and "wrongs." Many of these are sound and beneficial as evidenced by the fact that many have also been transformed into communal laws that are enforced for the benefit of the masses. However, many are also the product of attempts to control the masses, to further promote the respective religion, and ultimately, to benefit the leaders of that religion. It is difficult to put right and wrong aside. Imagine the chaos, the loss of serenity, the loss of compassion.

Faith is a wonderful thing when it is used to be spiritual and kind. It can bring us peace and joy when it is internalized along with acceptance for what others may believe. When we accept others' right to believe differently, we remove all negativity from faith. Faith can only have a component of hate and misery if we are angry at others for believing differently than we do and we feel a need to change everyone to believe the same as we do. There is no peace in that.

These writings are not intended to discredit these concepts. For some unknown reason, we feel "right" when we believe we are doing right. And "right," when it promotes the health and welfare of our species, our progress, our children's futures, is logical and welcomed. It is only the process of understanding where our concepts originate that is important in this discussion. Understanding what parameters and limitations are here for us, which ones we create of our own accord, and which ones we have the power to change is critical in understanding our own purpose and existence. In a way, we can create our own definitions of right and wrong based on our learning and our spirituality. But in the end, if we comprehend our own instinctive programming and the reasons behind it, we can become kinder and more reasonable people, even in strict adherence to our own faiths. As long as we are accepting of others and their right to believe what they believe, any benevolent belief system should operate to serve us.

CHAPTER 17

KINDNESS AND HATRED

Human beings are naturally tribal. We tend to group together as a common tribe, whether based on family, geography, ethnicity, religion or a multitude of other commonality factors. And as we are part of the tribe, we are programmed to see "others" outside our tribe as the enemy and we bestow our hatred on them.

Why? Maybe we are programmed that way so natural selection works more efficiently. Presumably, the stronger, smarter, more advanced tribe will wipe out the weaker lesser tribe and eliminate a less effective iteration in evolution and strengthen the surviving tribe. Whatever the reason, it is within the human condition. So, we tend to hate. We hate our "enemies," some for good reason, others often for just being different from us.

Hate is an interesting emotion. It must have some rational application, maybe as suggested above, but it is largely a self-harming emotion. When we hate, *we* suffer. Our stress level increases. We are bitter and we smile less. Simply put, we are less happy the more we hate. And as we live in a world where the rule of law and our ways of implementing justice largely control how we turn our hate into action, most of the targets of our hatred tend to continue their lives both oblivious to our hate and mostly unaffected by it. Unless we act on our hatred and take negative physical actions against our nemeses, putting ourselves in legal jeopardy, we end up taking a much, much greater toll on ourselves when we hate. Hate is a poison that we grow within ourselves.

Is there a solution? We largely can't control this wild feeling. It overtakes us. It consumes us. Like many other discussions above, it is not an easy solution and it comes with hard work and effort. But if we are successful even in *reducing* the hate we feel, the results are truly worthy. We need to start by identifying and acknowledging hatred as a self-harming emotion. And then, we need to learn to let it go. When someone has truly done us wrong, we can still harbor caution and avoidance, but we need to let the anger and hate subside within us and replace it with a more rationale methodology, such as by learning from the experience.

Unfortunately, a generally predominant reason for our hatred is based on a distaste and distrust of "others" unlike ourselves or those with different thoughts and beliefs. Simply by becoming more accepting and tolerant people, this source of hatred and anger will naturally subside. We need to work on being less judgmental. By allowing others to believe as they wish and actually respecting their right to be who they choose to be, or happen to be by nature, we benefit ourselves. We both reduce within ourselves the sting of this internal self-damaging poison and we become more apt to learn from that openness as we give respect and credence to other people's points of view. The hatred that is based on our differences and not on an individual's direct action is addressable by changing our own overall attitudes and judgments.

Sometimes there is good reason for our anger and hatred. Someone has done us wrong physically, financially, or attacking our character, among other reasons. Whatever the wrong may be, again, we primarily punish ourselves by feeling strong hatred. It's truly a difficult task to let this type of anger go. It takes active realization that we are feeling a negative emotion and it is damaging us. It takes long term effort and focus to slowly lessen the feelings and let "karma" take its course. Usually, wrongdoers end up paying a rather large price as they rarely can experience the calm and contentment of a clear conscious. By focusing on slowly relinquishing our anger, we will lessen the stress and damage we are experiencing, enabling us to enjoy our lives more fully.

On the opposite end of the spectrum is our emotion of compassion and kindness. When my father was a young man, his closest friend and partner in business passed away unexpectedly. He was devastated. A few nights later, the friend appeared in my father's dream unusually vividly. He told my father that he had "come back" to let him know that the "purpose of life was *kindness.*" My father didn't quite understand the dream until many weeks later when he remembered a conversation with his partner before his partner passed away where they had discussed life and death and the purpose of life. In this conversation, they casually agreed that the first to pass away would come back, if they could, and tell the other what they had learned of the purpose of life. The conversation had not stuck with my father and he had not remembered it until after the dream. My father's story always stayed with me. I'm not sure it's evidence of an afterlife; I still just don't know. It does, however, make one think of the possibilities. Although it clearly could have been a creation of the subconscious mind, nonetheless, it made me think long and hard about the mysteries of life.

We can readily see why the quality of kindness is instilled in the human condition. And as before, it is an emotion more predominant when our lives are more fulfilled and our stomachs satiated. But it is part of the tribal nature of mankind to bond with those like ourselves. And so we tend to limit our kindness to those we have a bond with. As we become more learned and wise, we also tend to be kinder toward others, even those outside our circles. Unlike hatred, it is an emotion that brings great internal benefit as it is doled out to others. We receive a sense of satisfaction and harmony as we give kindness. Dispensing it hardly costs us anything but the rewards are great. It makes us happier people.

In this reality, it is possible we are seeing evidence of our Creator's intentions and goals with respect to the human race. Maybe we truly are here to grow to a point where harmony and kindness are the results of our advancement. Kindness doesn't have to be a grand act. Although the grand acts give us grander satisfaction, a simple smile to a stranger is also kindness. A wave at a small child. If we strive to be more kind, we will find more happiness.

Other than for the selfish reason of bettering our own lives, kindness has great communal benefits as well. It's a contagious emotional response. As we act out on kindness, the recipient of that kindness is more compelled to also show kindness to others. As kindness flows in a group or society, it makes all its participants kinder and happier. Looking at our societies on earth today, it is readily apparent that the more advanced, more prosperous populations contain more kindness and general good will toward others. It's apparent in the value we put on pets. How we care for wildlife and how we care for our own less fortunate and those in other nations. It's a clear pattern. Our lives are better when we are kinder, both as individuals and as communities. It hardly matters which order is the cause and effect. Kindness is a sign of progress and advanced intelligence. That doesn't mean to say kindness doesn't exist in less educated and less prosperous populations. It certainly does. People with less often have more empathy than those with more. But I believe by our very natures, kindness is directly attached to our progress as a species.

So, maybe kindness is, to some extent, incorporated into the purpose of life. If we believe we are here to learn and to better our race, maybe there's a connection. We incorporate more kindness in our lives when we have learned to overcome our lesser emotions and have advanced in our knowledge. The more we better ourselves, the more kindness exists in our communities. Whatever one believes in this area, it is clear that kindness is a powerfully positive component of our lives. And something that should be exercised often and freely. For our own sake.

CHAPTER 18

THE GIFT OF LIFE

Have you ever thought what a miracle it was that *you* were born? You won the lottery, only you don't know it. Consider the odds of your parents getting together (even consider the odds that *they* were born), the odds that they took the actions that created your life at the exact time that would require you to be conceived. The odds that the only sperm that would be you, out of the millions that raced to the only egg that could be you, made it first to the finish line. The moment you were conceived, a great gift was bestowed upon you that was denied trillions of other potential lives. You were born a winner. Since you invested nothing in this equation, your life is a very, very special gift. What exactly is this gift? It is a finite amount of time. Only for you, to be you. To walk this earth, to experience its beauty and bounty, to partake of its challenges, to taste, to feel, to touch the face of humanity. You are thrust onto a scene and given tools to make your mark, to live a life. If we tried to count the ways with which we often waste this gift, we would spend an eternity.

If we can adjust our attitude and our perception of everything that happens to us in our life, we can become much happier people. We need to start with acknowledging what a great gift we hold. There are some very negative experiences in our lives that are very difficult to trivialize and to remove our pain, like losing a loved one. But almost everything else depends greatly on how we view the "negative" events in our lives. When confronted with a great difficulty, I often ask myself, "What will it matter in a hundred years?" I'll be gone. Pretty much everyone I know will be gone. What meaning will this event have then? Who will care? We can fret and dwell in the pain or we can take it as another negative experience life will always bestow upon us at various times in our lives and actively weigh it against all the positive things in our life. Good people, true friends, our pets, the beauty of nature, the very fact that we are here, today, to take on challenges.... When we start thinking this way, it becomes clearer that there will always be difficulties and challenges but when weighed against the good and positive of our lives, the scales weigh heavily in favor of the good. With this new perspective, we can deal with negative experiences with less grief and pain.

Again, going back to attitude, if we adjust how we view things and how catastrophic we allow our perspective of a negative experience to be, we will find we have tremendous control over our own happiness. Life is a gift. It is a short, limited amount of time. As much as possible, we should never let anything sour even a single day. If we put the event, the difficulty, the challenge in a "box" and take on the attitude: "I can handle it; I will do my best to fix it but I will not let it ruin this day which is a precious day in my limited life or let it affect my appreciation of all the good in my life," we will find, slowly, over time, our perspective will change, we will handle all challenges better, and we will become happier people overall.

The natural reaction is that it's not that easy. And sometimes it's not. There are certain times when I've had such challenges with health issues affecting loved ones that I found it truly hard to be grateful and carry a positive attitude. The pain can occasionally be overwhelming. In such cases, I still persisted to weigh each and every positive thing in my life against the current challenge. It wasn't easy and it certainly didn't end my distress. But it helped. There's *always* worse and there's always something we can find that can offset the pain. Especially when we take into consideration all the positives we are experiencing, including the fact that we even have the ailing individual in our lives in the first place.

As previously discussed, a side component of this attitude change is learning to be grateful. We usually spend our lives taking for granted all the great, wonderful gifts we have and making mountains of our problems. If we put things in true and proper perspective, normally, we all will find that the good in our lives greatly exceeds the negative by a large margin. Just remember to be grateful for all the positive things in your life on a daily basis. And to review as many of them as you can think of every day. This will make you more aware of them and bring you a step closer to more happiness.

Having been given this gift of life, what should we do with it? It is a limited precious commodity. Your journey on earth is a temporary visit and then you will no longer be here. This gift of time is often confusing. It's difficult for us to comprehend. How can *we* not exist? As discussed, it is beyond our core mental ability to deeply understand that we are no more than a short-lived link in the chain of humanity.

This gift of time is shared with our contemporaries and in little over a century not one of us will still be here. We will have been a foregone notion in time, a lost link in the chain. The point is not to stress you out over the prospect of non-existence. It is to help you understand and appreciate the greatness and magnitude of the gift you're currently experiencing. We can only appreciate that which we have, when we have a reference for *not* having it. And of course, we always have life as long as we are thinking. But our wonderful mind has the ability, with some effort, to fill in the blank and create a realm out of nonexistence with which to compare the joy of being. If we truly realize and recognize deeply that life is a finite gift, we will engage on our expenditures of time more fruitfully and with a better perspective.

CHAPTER 19

WE ARE OUR OWN MASTERS

So, what is "real happiness"? It goes right back to attitude and gratitude. Real happiness is when we realize and appreciate all the positives in our lives overall even when we have great challenges to happiness before us. Real happiness is when we learn to take the negative in stride since there will always be negatives to deal with. We can better take the negatives in stride with a view toward balancing and weighting the situation against the good and positive factors in our lives and find gratitude even in the face of adversity. I believe *that* is the foundation for regular and continuous, true happiness.

Realization or an awakening is what it really takes. For all these concepts are in reality simply "seeing" what is already there. It is not creating or building new concepts but rather finding realization that truths exist that we have become numb to. There is so much good we have become blind to. There is so much we can adjust in our own minds that will make a great difference in our lives. There is so much peace and contentment waiting to be realized by fine-tuning our own minds. Realization is not a momentary occurrence in this context. We don't just think about it and jump into a state of awakening. It is a process. A process of thoughtful consideration, a process of acknowledging certain realities that have been taken for granted on a regular basis, and adjusting our attitudes accordingly. Again, these concepts take work and effort, but in the end they result in a state that leads to a more content existence.

The great gift of life is a gift of time. We all spend our lives trying to learn more, gain more, and progress. But at the end of it all, we are left with the same bareness we entered the world with. We leave with nothing. So, when we're done, what did it all mean? Hopefully we left the world a little better than when we found it. By any little contribution. Even if it was simply just leaving others behind that benefitted from our guidance and love. But more importantly, how much happiness did we experience in our journey of time? How much did we appreciate the joy of life?

I hope that if I can have rational thought at the end of my life, I will be able to look back and not have any regrets. That would be a life well lived. To me that largely depends on how happy I was and how much kindness and goodwill I spread during my time on this beautiful and amazing planet.

There are many secrets to being happier. Above are those I have found to be the most powerful. A sense of balance in our lives, a good attitude about life, gratitude for all the good in our lives, less hatred and anger and more kindness… these are a few key factors. We humans have a great ability to modify our states of mind by deliberate reflection. As we learn and grow, we are also finding new ways to master our own mental outlooks, to become "better" people, happier people and a more advanced and sophisticated species of life. As each of us becomes more and more a master of our own emotional and rational outlook, as we alter our human condition, we become a better community of humanity.

We have the ability to look upon ourselves from a broader and wider perspective. To stand outside our personal "realities" we experience through our physical circumstances and judge the world from a fact-based viewpoint. Doing so gives us the ability to look upon our own human condition, the parameters we are endowed with, and adjust our thoughts and behavior to better ourselves.

Like anything else in life, good things require a little bit of effort. What greater reward can we hope for than to lead happier lives? It is a worthy effort to work on our own daily happiness. Let's not live our lives to be happy in the future. Now is the only real and tangible time in your life. The past is just memories in our minds. A foundation of learning and experiences to build on today. Other than that, it doesn't exist. It is only in our minds. *Today* is your life. *Now* is what you build into the foundations of your memories, which make up who you are. Now is your expenditure of your limited time on earth. Now is what you will look back on when you gauge the success of your life. Tomorrow needs to be planned, but it is just a promise, one that *may* never come. So today *is* your life. Live life to feel happiness in the "now" of it all.

Printed in the United States
by Baker & Taylor Publisher Services